THE HUNGRY YEARS

PARADIS, ADRIAN A

THE HUNGRY YEARS
THE STORY OF THE
GREAT AMERICAN
DEPRESSION

THE
HUNGRY
YEARS

THE STORY OF
THE GREAT
AMERICAN
DEPRESSION

Adrian A. Paradis

CHILTON BOOK COMPANY

Philadelphia   New York   London

To the Reader

"Dad, what was the depression?"

By the time each of our three children had asked this question, I realized that there was a large gap in their knowledge of recent history. Anyone who grew up during the prosperous period following World War II, and did not live through those hungry years of the nineteen-thirties, could never really envision what it was like to live through a depression.

There was nothing unique about the depression that commenced in 1930. It was not the first one in America—there had been nineteen depressions before it came along, starting with that of 1785–1789. None of the previous depressions, however, had affected so many Americans so drastically.

A bit of advice that appeared in a Connecticut newspaper during the depression of 1819–1820 should have been reprinted just prior to the depression of the nineteen-thirties:

> *Why is the community so much embarrassed?*
> *Because banks lend money that they have not got to lend*
> *And because people spend money they have not got to spend.*
> ### REMEDY
> *Own the money before you lend it!*
> *Earn the money before you spend it!*

What Was the Depression?

It was a time when almost fifteen million workers could not find jobs and unemployed men and women sold apples on street corners. Some people starved to death. Others shivered in cardboard shacks. Like hoboes, thousands of young people roamed the country in freight cars. Numerous tragic bank failures ended in the temporary closing of every bank in the United States by proclamation of President Franklin D. Roosevelt.

Such was the great depression of the nineteen-thirties, an almost unbelievable chapter in America's history. Probably no other event has changed our way of living so greatly or affected the nation's future to such an extent. This book was written about those hungry years because every American who did not live through that period should know about it.

Today many of us take our privileges for granted, but it was not many years ago that men who joined labor unions lost their jobs. Americans who were sick or hungry had no place to turn for help. The elderly who had been unable to save for retirement had no place to live, and most of those who lost their jobs soon became destitute. Guarantees of rights for workingmen, welfare payments, medicare, social security, unemployment insurance—these, and many other benefits we now enjoy and take for granted, can be traced back to those desperate years.

Life was difficult then for millions of men and women, but they did not give up. Babies were born, teen-agers went to college and found jobs, young people married and started families. A few people made a lot of money, many had nothing, some experienced no real change in their living standards. There were heroes and heroines who dedicated their lives to helping less fortunate neighbors. It was a period that taxed and tested American ingenuity and courage, but the nation emerged from the depression fighting and victorious, and in many ways better for the experience.

How America solved its problems is a story of pluck, of determination to succeed in spite of disaster, and of courage to face the future. It is a drama that is peculiarly American. It bears telling again, not only to those who may have forgotten the past but especially to those young Americans who have never known what it is to be hungry, without work, without hope. Because the depression helped shape our American heritage, familiarity with what happened during those hungry years should give you a new understanding as well as a deeper appreciation of the advantages, opportunities, and securities that America offers today.

I have not attempted to tell the whole story of the depression because that would require many volumes. Instead, I have tried to give some impression of what happened during those years, what it was like to live through them, and to cover the more important events. If you are interested in learning more about that period, I invite you to consult some of the books listed under *Suggested Readings* at the end of this book.

The Author

Contents

PART I
The Gathering Storm

The people who lined our avenues in 1919 to cheer the soldiers returning from the European battlefields rejoiced that the Armistice had halted the worst war the world had ever known. What they did not know was that this same merciful Armistice marked the beginning of a postwar period destined to end in 1930 with a disastrous world-wide depression.

The first section of this book deals with events that occurred during the postwar period and helped create the great depression here in America. The following highlights may refresh the reader's memory with respect to the years covered in the first three chapters.

EVENTS OF *1918–1929*

1918 Armistice ends World War I
1919 Start of speculative boom in the United States
Peace Conference in Paris
1920 Boom continues in America except for collapse of farm prices
Establishment of League of Nations
1921 General recession in the United States but start of depression for farmers
1922 Start of economic recovery in the United States
1924 Calvin Coolidge elected President of the United States
Florida real estate boom becomes widespread
Dawes Reparation Plan accepted by the Allies and Germany
1926 End of the Florida boom
1927 Start of the big bull market on the New York Stock Exchange
1928 Herbert Hoover elected President of the United States
1929 The October stock market crash

1

END OF AN ERA

Peter Grove of Cleveland arrived in Miami one morning during the spring of 1925 and walked from the railroad station to Flagler Street, the city's main thoroughfare. Like thousands of others, he had come to make a fortune in Florida real estate.

The city hummed with activity. The constant *tat-tat-tat* of riveters fastening the steel girders of the rising sky-scrapers made it difficult to be heard. Bumper-to-bumper traffic snarled every street corner and crept at a slow pace. Excited men and women crowded the sidewalks and jammed the real estate offices.

"Just one more seat in the big free bus. It's yours, friend!" A ruddy stout man grabbed Mr. Grove's arm.

"Here's your chance to see how the canals are dredged and the land beautified. We'll stop long enough at the office so you can pick up some real bargains."

"Not yet," Mr. Grove said. "I've got to find a hotel room first."

The bus driver shook his head sadly. "You won't find one, friend. People been sleeping in the station, in hotel lobbies—even their cars. This city's full up. Don't waste your time on that. Hop in the bus!"

Anxious as he was to inspect and buy property, Mr. Grove was more concerned with finding a place to sleep, so he walked on. A few minutes later, a man carrying a huge blueprint under his arm stopped him.

"Can I show you some excellent lots for sale?" Without waiting for an answer, he unrolled the blueprint and started to extol the virtues of his development.

"Hey! Stop that!" a burly policeman yelled. "Don't you know it's against the law to do business on the street or even show a map? Now get moving!"

The man and the map disappeared into the crowd and Mr. Grove decided that it would be wiser to do business with an established real estate broker. He saw a sign two doors away and went in. Here he was promised not only a couch to sleep on that night, but one of Florida's best buys in a brand new development called Manhattan Estates.

"It's not more than about three-quarters of a mile from the fast-growing, prosperous city of Nettie," the salesman assured Mr. Grove, as he wrote out a receipt for his binder of a hundred dollars. "I know you'll be very happy there."

Fortunately, Mr. Grove never learned whether or not he could be happy in Manhattan Estates. He found a buyer for his binder and doubled his money in the transaction.

Thus he did not know that there never had been a city called Nettie and that it was only the name of an abandoned turpentine camp.

In the immediately previous years Americans from every state had supported the most frenzied real estate boom the country had ever known. The speculative fever spread up and down the sandy Florida coasts as promoters vied with one another for purchasers. In Miami alone there were some two thousand real estate offices and twenty-five thousand agents rushing about pell-mell selling everything from house lots on beautiful Bay Biscayne to worthless and inaccessible acreage that lay under water.

The trick of making money was easy. First you decided which of the developments artistically pictured in colorful folders would make the best investment. Then you put down a binder of 10 per cent on the lot, turned around, and before the first payment became due thirty days later, sold it at a handsome profit. You reinvested your gain in other binders, always confident that you could sell the property—and make money. Under this system land values soared to ridiculous heights until midsummer of 1926. Then the buyers who were previously anxious to purchase property mysteriously disappeared, frightened away by the crazily inflated prices. Those who held binders were no longer able to sell them, and since they could not meet the payments on their lots the boom quickly died.

As if this were not enough tragedy to afflict Miami, the "Fair White Goddess of Cities"; Fort Lauderdale, "The Tropical Wonderland"; or Sanford, "The City Substantial"; and all the other glorious homesites both above and below water, further disaster was destined to strike the fabled peninsula. Early in the morning of September

18, 1926, a howling tropical storm that had gathered its fury in the West Indies slammed into Miami and then whistled its destructive way across the Sunshine peninsula. In its wake it left some four hundred dead, sixty-three hundred injured, and over fifty thousand homeless. Not only did the storm cause property damage that ran into the millions, but it also put the finishing touches to the famous Florida boom.

Two years after the hurricane Henry S. Villard, writing in *The Nation*, reported his impressions as he drove into Miami:

> Dead subdivisions line the highway, their pompous names half-obliterated on crumbling stucco gates. Lonely white-way lights stand guard over miles of cement sidewalks, where grass and palmetto take the place of homes that were to be. . . . Whole sections of outlying subdivisions are composed of unoccupied houses, past which one speeds on broad thoroughfares as if traversing a city in the grip of death.

Neither discouraged nor wiser for their experience, those Americans who thrived on speculation joined others who had dabbled in real estate developments elsewhere in the country and merely turned to another form of gambling, the stock market. Here 10 per cent margins took the place of 10 per cent binders as men and women bought huge blocks of stock, again confident that prices would continue to rise. And why not? It was an era of prosperity whose slogans included: "Two cars in every garage," "A chicken in every pot." War was behind the nation, a great future lay ahead as business kept growing, as the rich grew richer, and on all sides more and more people seemed to share the abundance of this great land of plenty.

Paradoxically, all was not as it appeared. Long before Black Thursday, October 24, 1929—the day that the bottom fell out of the stock market—over a million were unemployed and there were many signs that the economy was slowing down, but most Americans refused to believe that the New Era would ever come to an end. When the stock market crashed it did not cause the depression, but, like the opening game of the baseball season, heralded its start, acting as the spark that set off a series of damaging explosions.

2

SOME CAUSES OF THE DEPRESSION

Our depression was part of a world-wide collapse brought on by World War I, a war which gave rise to nationalism and the erecting of high tariff walls that restricted international trade.

Most countries experienced no strong recovery following the war. Germany, for instance, was required to pay such heavy reparations to the Allies after the peace treaty was signed that her recovery was impeded and she could not resume normal trading with her prewar customers. The Communist revolution of 1919 practically isolated Russia from other nations and eliminated her from the world marketplace.

There was unrest in many places as revolution and the

threat of revolution added to uncertainty and endangered American investments abroad. Depression had come to other nations before October, 1929, when our market crashed. Some of the countries which had already felt an economic recession were Australia, Bolivia, Brazil, Belgium, Germany, and India, while another half-dozen nations were already experiencing the effects of the first stages of recession.

No two economists or historians agree on all the causes responsible for those disastrous years, but there has been fairly general agreement that the following factors contributed to the calamity in the United States.

Diminished Business Activity

The stock market did not crash until October, 1929, but looking back we can see that the prosperous New Era, as the late nineteen-twenties were popularly called, began to lose its head of steam some time before Black Thursday. What happened at the National Utensil Company was typical of many manufacturing companies.

THE CUTBACK

"Hey, Maxel! Mr. Roberts wants to see you."

Henry Maxel hurried into the vice president's office and waited as Mr. Roberts thoughtfully chewed on his short cigar for a moment before he spoke

"Fire three hundred men this Friday," he said suddenly, "and two hundred next. We're cutting production."

"Wh-what did you say?" Henry stammered.

The company had been earning a good profit and there had not been a layoff in fifteen years. Everywhere people were making fortunes in the stock market. He must have misunderstood Mr. Roberts.

The vice president repeated the order.

"But why? What's wrong? What will I tell the men?"

"Tell 'em anything you want. The reason's simple—we've made more kitchen utensils than the ladies will buy. The warehouse is bulging with them. The stores aren't buying them any more. If you don't sell, there's no money coming in to pay wages. Does that answer your question?"

"I—I had no idea of this." Henry stared at the floor. He dreaded the unpleasant job ahead of him.

"It's not only us." Mr. Roberts chewed the cigar vigorously, then continued: "Manufacturers all over the country have been overproducing. Every week more and more are cutting back, trying to get to the point where they can sell what they make. Maybe it's part of the business cycle—I don't know. All I do know is we've got too many people on the payroll and it's up to you to get rid of them."

Meanwhile, stores had built up such large inventories of goods that they stopped ordering from the factories. When the market crash came, with many people losing all their savings and extra spending money, the demand dropped for goods which had piled up in stores and warehouses. Adding to the problem was the growing number of unemployed, whose purchasing stopped except for absolute necessities. Farmers too, millions of them, had little money and had been unable to do any buying for years. Little wonder the economy was in trouble!

The Plight of the Farmers

While the rest of the nation was enjoying Coolidge prosperity in the New Era, many farmers were living in privation, hopelessly in debt, and mortgaged with no possibility of ever regaining title to their property. Seemingly, no one was concerned.

"Farmers have never made money. I don't believe we can do much about it," President Coolidge told the chairman of the Farm Loan Board. In 1925–1926, farmers' cash receipts were only 40 per cent above the 1921 depression low point, but this proved to be the high point of the decade and thereafter income fell off. When Congress was asked to protect the farmer from foreign competition, as the protective tariff had shielded the manufacturer, there was little sympathetic response. Twice President Coolidge vetoed legislation that would have provided relief for destitute farmers.

To understand what happened to the farmers in the period immediately following World War I, consider the case of Martin Walker who owned a large farm in Iowa.

THE MAD SCRAMBLE FOR FARMS

Martin Walker had never been as well off as after the first World War in 1919. His corn, wheat, hay, hogs, and cattle brought high prices because he and all other farmers had to feed not only America but Europe as well. Thus the Walkers had been able to pay off their mortgage and even put a little money in the bank.

One day a tall stranger drove up in a new Model-T Ford. He was dressed smartly and wore a gray derby.

"Mr. Walker?" he asked, as he picked his way carefully

across the barnyard. "I'm Tom Goodwin, from the East. Interested in selling some land?"

"Don't know that I am, don't know that I'm not." Mr. Walker had never thought of selling any of his acreage. It had been in the family for generations, but no one had ever offered to buy it before.

"What do you want with it?" he asked, studying the stranger suspiciously.

"I'm interested in investing my money in farm lands out here. Crops and cattle are bringing such good prices, land should make a good investment."

"Come on in and we'll talk it over with the Missus." Mr. Walker led the way toward the house

An hour later he had signed a contract which gave Mr. Goodwin an option to buy two hundred acres for $20,000 within sixty days. Mr. Goodwin gave him a check for $2,000 and told him that if he did not pay up the balance of $18,000 before the option expired, he could keep the payment.

A week later, Gus Becker of the local bank dropped by and asked Mr. Walker to show him the land that Mr. Goodwin had bought. Together they drove out into the far pasture.

"Looks all right to me," Gus said, as they returned to the farmhouse. "We'll give him a mortgage for the balance due if he wants it, or we'll give it to somebody else. Never thought your land would be so valuable, eh, Martin?"

"But why are they buying it?" the farmer wanted to know. "It's the poorest piece we have. That's why I let him have it. You can't grow much on it."

The banker laughed. "They don't care whether it's good land or bad. Neither do we, as long as they pay their interest. All they want is to hold on for a week or two and sell that option. Then the new buyer will either get a big mortgage from us, or, if he's lucky, he'll renew the option and unload it on somebody else—at a profit, of course." He looked at Mr. Walker and winked. "Martin, here's your chance to make some real money."

"By golly, you're right," Mr. Walker admitted, thinking that this would be a far easier way to make a living than getting up at five and working until sundown.

With his two thousand dollars Mr. Walker purchased options on two nearby farms that were for sale, paying a thousand dollars down on each. Within a week he had sold one of the options for $1,500 and the other for $1,400. Immediately he reinvested the money by taking options on other farms.

"Looks like everybody's doing it," he told his wife one evening. "Barbers, grocers, teachers, butchers, clerks, farmers—everyone's in the game. The countryside's full of them, buying and selling options and land like crazy. It's getting harder to find farms with so many people looking for them."

"But Martin, you're paying awfully high prices for those options," Mrs. Walker observed. "They can't be worth it."

Mr. Walker smiled. He had learned a great deal during the past few weeks and had become as shrewd as "those city slickers from New York."

"Of course the farms aren't worth those prices," he agreed, "but I only pay for an option. I never really buy the land, and anyway, all I do is sell out to someone else at a profit."

"But suppose nobody wants to buy? Suppose the whole mad thing collapses? Then what?"

"Don't worry. I'll get out before that happens and we'll be rich the rest of our lives. As long as we farmers are getting high prices for our crops—and remember, we still have that income—people will want these farm lands and they'll keep buying options."

"Just the same, I wish you hadn't gotten another big mortgage on the farm so you could use that money to buy still more options. Doesn't make sense to me."

"Now don't you worry any more. I know what I'm doing. We'll be rich yet."

Like so many other Americans, Martin Walker was caught up in the contagious desire for personal gain which created a gambler's dream of making money quickly regardless of how it might hurt others—and in the long run, himself!

But Mr. Walker and thousands of other speculators in the Middle West were so busy searching for property, taking big mortgages, and buying and selling options on farms, that they had no time to study farm trends or observe what was happening in Europe.

After the armies were mustered out in 1919, the European farmers returned to their fields. Soon they were producing so well that the market for American farm products began to drop. Prices for our farmers' produce continued to fall, but no one bothered to notice.

Then one day in 1921 Mr. Walker discovered that there was not a single buyer for any of the options he held. Checking at the bank, he found that option prices had dropped overnight. No one wanted to invest in them.

"Your crops won't bring enough money to pay next year's taxes, Martin," Gus Becker said. "Who wants farm lands? The bubble has burst and there's going to be the dickens to pay."

The Walkers soon learned how right Gus was. The options they held on farms proved to be worthless, and, since they had no money to purchase the properties, they lost all the cash they had paid for the options. Their own crops brought so little money that they quickly fell behind in paying the monthly installments on the mortgage. Soon Gus was back at the farm.

"Hate to tell old friends like you bad news," he said, as he scratched his arm nervously and looked across the fields. "But we'll have to foreclose unless you can catch up on your payments."

Tears filled Mrs. Walker's eyes. This farm had been her great-grandfather's. It had always served the family well, and now it would no longer be theirs. It made her feel dizzy and sick, but she said nothing.

After a long silence Mr. Walker spoke. "It's no use." His voice was almost a whisper. "We're wiped out clean as a whistle."

A year later weeds grew high about the abandoned old farmhouse. The family had moved to the city where Mr. Walker found a job and started life anew. Gus Becker was gone, too, because his bank, like hundreds of others which held large worthless mortgages on farms, had failed and closed its doors.

Fortunately, all the banks and all the farmers were not caught up in the 1921 debacle. Many farmers remained in business, and those who gradually tried to farm more efficiently through the use of machines found that, although they could produce at less cost, they were soon creating for themselves and other farmers a new problem—overproduction.

In 1926, the corn crop increased over the previous year's production by six hundred million bushels but decreased in value by three hundred million dollars! The same thing happened to other farm products. Thus the depressed condition of the majority of our farmers proved such a drag on the economy that eventually it became one of the forces that helped turn our prosperity into depression.

Wealth Concentrated in the Hands of a Few

The old-fashioned virtue of thrift gave place to the new cult of installment buying. Americans discovered that it was now possible to heed the call of the hucksters because a man's purchasing ability was no longer limited by the size of his bank balance. The way was open for new sales promotions and campaigns that helped to broaden markets, step up industrial production, and give business new vitality.

Prosperity was not shared by everyone, however. We have already noted the farmers' plight. Textiles, lumber, and leather were among industries which seemed to have slumped into a continuous state of depression. Even during the boom years the average number of unemployed ran to a million and a half, and neither wage earners nor salaried workers were becoming rich. After 1923, real wages remained practically stationary and unemployment caused by technological advances increased each year.

The tragic fact was that most Americans were really poor. Six out of every ten families had incomes of less than $2,000 a year, a sum which permitted them to buy only the most basic necessities of life. Only three out of every hundred families had incomes of over $10,000 a year, and it was this small group of wealthy individuals who provided much of the money needed for investments in new plants. They spent most of their money on food, rent, and clothing, and provided the cash that supported the producers of luxury goods. Thus, as soon as this small sector of our population was hit by the stock market crash, they stopped buying luxuries and cut off the flow of funds on which business had depended greatly.

Holding Companies

In 1929, few people were aware of how many holding companies existed in the United States, or the power which they wielded. A holding company is exactly what the name implies: it holds the ownership of other corporations and may provide over-all direction and management to its subsidiary companies whose stock it holds. Today the largest and best-known is the American Telephone and Telegraph Company, which owns the stock of numerous local telephone companies and provides over-all direction to them.*

During the nineteen-twenties, ingenious financiers, some honest and many otherwise, used the holding company device to put together vast empires, principally in the entertainment, railroad, and utility fields. One of the largest, and called "the world's safest investment," was the creation of English-born Samuel Insull. Once Thomas A. Edison's private secretary, he became a Chicago millionaire stock manipulator who dominated Chicago's political and social circles for many years. He built a reputation for being trustworthy. He also created an intricate pyramid of public utility holding companies that attracted money from thousands of widows, pensioners, aged people, and others who invested their life savings

* American Telephone and Telegraph Company is also an operating company, inasmuch as it operates the long-distance telephone lines that connect the various separate companies.

in this gigantic enterprise. Insull's corporate manipulations and speculations with company funds brought about one of the greatest bankruptcies of all time. When the Insull system failed in 1932, it was worth almost three billion dollars and was producing an eighth of all the electric power in the United States.

In effect what happened was this: Stock manipulators established a top holding company by selling bonds and stocks and used the money they received to buy up enough stock of existing companies to control them. Whenever the promoters wanted to raise more money, they created a second holding company, which in turn would buy up the first, and later they might organize a third, and so on, until a crazy hodgepodge of companies was created.

After the stock market crashed, there were no more cash customers to buy the securities. More important, as the depression deepened, operating companies made less and less money, so that the holding companies were not getting enough cash to meet the huge interest payments on the bonds they had sold, and this caused them to collapse like houses of cards.

The holding companies took all their subsidiaries' earnings which normally were used to expand operations and to buy expensive equipment and machinery. This meant fewer orders for the factories and less employment, which, because of the size of the power industry, had a depressing effect on the economy. Little wonder that Congress eventually outlawed giant holding companies!

The Investment Trusts

Collapse of many investment trusts created additional hardship. Investment trusts had been invented many,

many years before 1929, but never had they become so popular nor so easy to start. An investment trust is an organization that invests its money in securities—stocks or bonds—of other companies. For its income it depends on the dividends and interest received from the securities it owns.

One reason for the popularity of investment trusts—or mutual funds, as many are now called—is that an investor who does not trust his judgment of stocks and bonds can purchase shares of an investment trust which employs trained analysts and economists to manage its funds. Investment trusts were popular between 1926 and 1929 because they made money as stocks kept rising in value. Since the public did not bother to investigate before it bought, promoters of investment trusts had a field day— that is, until the market crashed.

Testifying before a committee of the United States Senate, Mr. Sachs, of Goldman Sachs & Company, stated in 1932 that his company had organized an investment trust, the Goldman Sachs Trading Corporation. Senator Couzens asked at what price the stock was sold.

MR. SACHS: At $104.
SENATOR COUZENS: And what is the price of the stock now?
MR. SACHS: Approximately $1.75.

The Weak Banking System

Following the mid-Twenties, there was an increasing number of foreclosures on farms as mortgages became due and farmers were unable to pay. Banks found themselves loaded with unsalable property, which resulted in numerous failures. During the 1926–1928 years, 1,588 banks with deposits totaling $539,000,000 closed their doors.

Officers of stronger banks learned nothing from the numerous bank failures. They fell into the same trap by overextending credit, making loans on securities that were constantly rising in paper value only and on urban real estate which was enjoying a boom of its own.

Although bank closings during the Twenties did not bring on the depression, they were symptomatic of the precarious condition of the entire banking structure. It was inevitable, therefore, that, when the boom collapsed in 1929, many of the banks which had extended credit beyond reasonable limits were bound to suffer and contribute to the economic depression. Blame for the rash of bank closings should not be laid entirely on the bankers who were often overeager to lend other people's money. Much of the fault could be laid at the door of the Federal Reserve Board, which was expected to set the banking tone for the nation.

Federal Reserve Policies

As Secretary of Commerce, Herbert Hoover repeatedly warned against the policies of the Federal Reserve Board, whose members (with one exception) Hoover described as "mediocrities."

"The Reserve policies . . . mean inflation with inevitable collapse which will bring calamities upon our farmers, our workers and legitimate business," Mr. Hoover said.

On the other hand, Roy Young, governor of the Federal Reserve Board, was said to have been laughing as he watched the rising prices on the ticker tape.

"What I am laughing at," he said, "is that I am sitting here trying to keep a hundred and twenty million people from doing what they want to do!"

In March, 1929, when President Coolidge left office, he dismissed the stock market with the happy comment that stocks were "cheap at current prices," and the country was "absolutely sound." It was not his responsibility to regulate the boom but up to the Federal Reserve Board, which Congress had created as a strong central bank. However, that group, many of whose members were profiting from the boom, was not about to do anything that would disturb the status quo. They felt that it could be as dangerous to curb the speculation and risk a bust as it was to let it march on unchecked. The latter seemed the more sensible course of action.

Holding the power to stop the headlong rush into disaster by increasing the rediscount rates, the governors hesitated, drew back, and stood by helplessly while one of their members—Charles Mitchell, chairman of the influential National City Bank of New York—announced that his bank was ready to lend money to all who cared to come and apply for it.

Meanwhile, the public was coming in such numbers to buy stocks on margin that the New York banks could not supply all of the money needed. They soon became agents for other banks that wanted to share in the money making. Not content with the usual interest rate of 5 per cent, they found that, as the frenzy in the stock market increased, interest rates went up, up, up, until 12 per cent was reached. The smartest banks of all were those which turned around, borrowed at 5 per cent from the Federal Reserve Bank, then loaned the same funds at 12 per cent.

As stocks continued their upward march during 1929

and as interest rates grew higher and higher, the Federal Reserve System still remained silent except for a few innocuous and meaningless statements. If anyone was thought to be responsible for regulating the New York Stock Exchange, it was Governor Franklin D. Roosevelt of New York, since the Exchange was located within his state and no Federal law had been created to regulate it.

With the Federal Reserve Board looking the other way, with no government agency to curb the speculative orgy, with corporations, banks, and individuals ready to loan money to speculators at unheard-of interest rates as high as 20 per cent, the stage was set for the biggest and most spectacular economic bust the world had ever seen!

3

THE CRASH

It was cloudy over downtown Manhattan that Thursday morning, October 24, 1929, as the subways and elevated trains disgorged their thousands of passengers at the Wall Street stations. Many of the men and women were tired from working late the night before, but the overtime could come in handy and might even buy a good stock.

Before the bell rang at ten o'clock, some eleven hundred brokers—instead of the usual seven or eight hundred—were poised on the trading floor of the New York Stock Exchange, ready to handle the expected high trading volume. Extra girls manned the switchboards and every available Stock Exchange employee was on duty.

Newspaper headlines told the story of the previous day's disaster:

PRICES OF STOCK CRASH IN HEAVY LIQUIDATION
TOTAL DROP OF BILLIONS
PAPER LOSS $4,000,000,000
2,600,000 SHARES SOLD IN THE FINAL HOUR IN RECORD DECLINE—
MANY ACCOUNTS WIPED OUT
NO BROKERAGE HOUSE IN DIFFICULTIES AS MARGINS
HAVE BEEN KEPT HIGH
ORGANIZED BACKING ABSENT
BANKERS CONFER ON STEPS TO SUPPORT MARKET
HIGHEST BREAK IS 96 POINTS

Employees of brokerage houses had worked late that night, accounting for the record six million shares traded. Brokers asked one another what in the world was happening? It was the largest break in the market for two years. Although everyone knew that prices were ridiculously inflated, hadn't Charles E. Mitchell, chairman of the big National City Bank, said that nothing was fundamentally wrong with the stock market or underlying business and the credit structure?

"The public is suffering from 'brokers' loanitis,' " the great man had proclaimed.

Right he was, for more than six billion dollars had poured into brokers' hands—at interest rates as high as 20 per cent—to be loaned to greedy, reckless gamblers. Speculators, who discovered that margin was magic, lost no time using it. Thus the man who bought stock on margin had all the benefits of ownership, including dividends and increases in market value, merely by pledging the stock as collateral for the margin loan he received from his broker. A trader who paid two hundred dollars toward the purchase of securities worth a thousand dollars could borrow the balance of eight hundred dollars. As long as the market value of the stock went up, he was making money. But the moment it dropped to eight hundred dollars or below, the amount of his loan, he had to put up additional cash or the stock would be sold to satisfy the loan. Those who had gambled on a continuously rising market by putting all their cash into stocks and borrowing on margin were caught as the market fell. Unable to supply the needed funds, they stood by helplessly and watched their cash disappear as the prices tumbled.

Not all of the speculators or marginal operators had been cleaned out by Wednesday's market break, however. Brokers knew by the number of sell orders that were flooding their offices that Thursday would be just as bad.

Preparations had not been taken in vain, for the instant the Exchange opened an avalanche of selling orders descended to the trading floor. A block of twenty thousand shares of Kennecott Copper was sold, followed by twenty thousand shares of General Motors. Brokers fought to keep up with the terrific volume, but there were far too many orders to execute. Those who followed the stock ticker watched it fall behind at an alarming rate. Soon it became impossible to tell how the market was going or to learn the last sale price of a particular stock.

News of the runaway market spread quickly by word of mouth. Crowds jammed into narrow Wall Street. Motion picture cameramen took up positions on the steps of the Sub-Treasury Building across from the New York Stock Exchange. Wild rumors leaped from person to person—the Buffalo and Chicago exchanges had closed; banks had failed; eleven speculators had committed suicide; at that very moment ambulances were speeding to save men who had shot themselves; a workman standing on top of a nearby building was going to jump.

By half-past twelve a record number of 722 people had walked up to the Stock Exchange visitors' gallery. It was then cleared to permit Winston Churchill, Chancellor of the Exchequer of Great Britain, to witness the unprecedented and furious trading. Neither Churchill nor his hosts knew that they were present at not just the collapse of a long speculative boom but something vastly more important—the beginning of a new era that would bring hardship to millions, to be followed by sweeping economic and social reforms.

"The ticker is two hours and four minutes behind," someone informed the distinguished visitor. Indeed, the excitement on the floor was now at its peak, as brokers shouted in vain, trying to find buyers for stocks that were dumped to be "sold at market."

Across the street in the office of J. P. Morgan & Company, five of the country's foremost bankers were meeting: Charles E. Mitchell, chairman of the National City Bank; Albert H. Wiggin, chairman of the Chase National Bank; William Potter, president of the Guaranty Trust Company; Seward Prosser, chairman of the Bankers Trust Company; and Thomas W. Lamont, senior partner of the Morgan firm. After discussing briefly what, if anything, should be done to stem the tidal wave of selling orders, they authorized Mr. Lamont to speak on their behalf.

"There has been a little distress selling on the Stock Exchange," he told the newspaper reporters who expected an important statement, "and we have held a meeting of the heads of several financial institutions to discuss the situation. We have found that there are no houses in difficulty and reports from brokers indicate that margins are being maintained satisfactorily. . . . It is the consensus of the group that many of the quotations on the Stock Exchange did not fairly represent the situation."

Meanwhile, pandemonium had seized most brokerage offices. A deluge of sell orders from all parts of the world cascaded into the Wall Street district. Margin clerks, purchase clerks, order clerks, sales clerks, stenographers, runners, and even the partners—all were enmeshed in wild confusion. No broker had ever handled such a volume of business before. None was prepared to do so now.

There was no way anyone could tell at what prices stocks were selling once the ticker had failed to keep up with the terrific pace on the trading floor. To add to the confusion, it seemed as though every customer was telephoning for information and that those who could not place calls through the switchboards had crowded into the offices. If a frantic customer was fortunate, he might be able to grab a clerk who invariably carried a pile of papers in one hand and a sandwich in the other, but the pleading questions usually went unanswered.

"I haven't the slightest idea," was the best reply anyone could get or give.

About one-thirty, William Whitney, vice president of the Stock Exchange and a floor broker for J. P. Morgan & Company, pushed his way confidently through the mob on the trading floor of the Exchange to the post where steel was traded. He placed a bid for ten thousand shares, then proceeded to other posts where he placed orders for a dozen or more other stocks.

The gesture worked! Immediately word spread that the bankers had moved in to save the situation and prices started an upward spiral. Now speculators worried lest they could not get back in at prices low enough to make a good profit! The hypodermic soon wore off, however, for the rising trend turned downward again as a new wave of selling orders coming in from all parts of the country hit the market. Nevertheless, when the closing gong sounded at three, only a third of the previous day's losses had been registered by the *Times* industrial average.

Exhausted, harried brokers straggled back to their offices. Here they and every other available employee faced the almost impossible task of completing the necessary accounting and bookkeeping transactions to record every detail of the day's trading.

Although the market was now closed, most of the customers' rooms in brokerage houses were still crowded. Dazed by the steady downward march of prices, glassy-eyed speculators sat glumly until after dark, watching the illuminated strips of opaque glass over which passed the quotations of stock sales made hours before. Not until 7:08 P.M. did the final transaction, which had taken place at 3:00 P.M., move over the glass.

That night more than fifty thousand employees, pausing only for dinner, worked at a frenzied pace trying to tabulate the day's transactions. Hoards of workers descended on the few eating places that were still open, and restaurants which had been deserted throughout the day became so busy that they had to place emergency calls for provisions. Hotel rooms in the city were at a premium as brokerage firms engaged whole floors so that their employees would be able to get an hour or two of sleep. Messengers and office boys ran shouting and whooping through the dimly lighted streets as they carried securities from office to office. At eight-thirty several hundred boys burst from the Bankers Trust building and created such an uproar that police were called to disperse them.

Western Union offices, swamped with messages speeding to and from New York, shattered all previous records.
One large brokerage concern advised its customers to
keep their accounts well margined and recommended
that those "with available funds should take advantage
of this break to buy good securities." Other firms wired
their customers similar instructions, and practically every
house sent telegrams to certain customers demanding
more margin.

FAILURE TO COVER YOUR MARGIN WILL NECESSITATE
SELLING YOUR HOLDINGS WHEN MARKET OPENS

was the cheery news Western Union delivery boys took
to speculators in every part of the country.

Not so fortunate were the many small speculators who
dabbled in the market and had failed to cover their
stocks. Long after midnight, as the figures for Thursday's
trading were posted, account after account was marked
Closed and another would-be millionaire was eliminated.
In one firm a clerk found a basket crammed with sell
orders which had been overlooked during the day's hectic
business. It was too late to do anything but quietly toss
the messages into the trash.

Gradually the lights in the Wall Street canyon snapped
off as exhausted stenographers, clerks, department heads,
salesmen, and partners made their way home or to mid-
town hotels to catch an hour or two of rest before returning for the next day.

Friday was bad, too! It seemed as though every remaining owner of stock had at last panicked and decided
to unload his holdings at any price. Stocks cascaded into
the Exchange and prices skidded as blocks of securities

were offered for whatever they might bring. A record-breaking sixteen million shares changed hands with staggering losses for the sellers.

By the following Wednesday, despite a slight rebound, brokers were exhausted, records were hopelessly snarled, and nerves were so jangled that something had to be done to halt the madness. The Stock Exchange governors voted to close the Exchange for two days to give brokers a chance to catch up and straighten out their accounts.

"The organizations of the Stock Exchange houses have reached a point of complete physical exhaustion," the Board of Governors declared. (This was the first time the New York Stock Exchange had been closed since 1914, when World War I began.)

Stock Exchange officials hoped that the temporary closing of the market might help restore some semblance of order and trading sanity when it reopened, but not so! When the opening bell rang the following Monday, further violent selloffs continued to push prices down. Reluctantly, the Board of Governors voted to limit trading to three hours a day until further notice.

Meanwhile, from all sides came reassuring statements that the economy was sound and business was good. United States Steel Corporation declared an extra dividend of one dollar. One financial writer blamed the crash on selling by foreigners, whereas the Troy (New York) *Times* told its readers that the market crash "was a local disturbance." The Chicago *Evening Post* confidently stated that "prosperity will continue." President Herbert Hoover asserted that "the fundamental business of the country, that is, production and distribution of commodities, is on a sound and prosperous basis."

Indeed, the Federal Reserve Board found that no action on its part was necessary and a well-known bank official said that it was merely a security panic with paper losses. To show its faith in the future of America and help "assure a continuation of good business throughout the country," the Ford Motor Company slashed prices on all its cars, the largest cut being made on the standard coupé, which was reduced from $550.00 to $500.00.

Comedians had a good time with the stock market crash. One jokester advised people to carry an umbrella to protect themselves from all those distraught investors who were jumping out of windows from time to time. It was said that when people asked for rooms in New York hotels the clerks asked, "For sleeping or jumping?"

Almost every day newspapers carried stories of people who had committed suicide, men like the president of the Rochester Gas & Electric Corporation, whose losses in the stock market were estimated at $1,200,000 during a single month; the head of a wholesale produce firm; a woman in Washington, D. C.; or the president of the County Trust Company (of Westchester County, New York), whose death was kept quiet for twenty hours to avoid unduly alarming the bank's depositors.

More fortunate was Lawrence J. Fava, a Philadelphia real estate dealer, who became "frantic" over his losses and jumped into the Schuylkill River. The shock of the icy water quickly changed his mind and he managed to reach the shore safely. In spite of the publicity given these gruesome stories, the records do not indicate that there was any great increase in the suicide rate after the market crash.

By the middle of November, activity on the Exchange subsided as the month-long nightmare came to an end. Stunned by the magnitude of the Wall Street catastrophe, men and women everywhere found it unbelievable that the beautiful, foolproof machinery for making money was no longer there. It was impossible to grasp the fact that some thirty billion dollars of paper values had disappeared within a few weeks, that the business leadership of Wall Street was destroyed, and that the country's credit system had been badly damaged.

Now unemployment began to rise, and the signs were all too clear to the few discerning economists who understood what had really happened. The country had slid into what might rapidly become a serious and widespread depression—possibly, some said, the worst economic disaster in the nation's history.

PART II

The Years of Travail

Sooner or later, the depression touched the lives of most Americans in one way or another. The events of those years were so momentous and far-reaching that it would be impossible to record all of them within a book of this size. It is possible, however, to present a chronological story of the principal facts relating to the depression, as so many historians have done, but to understand what the depression meant to the people who lived through it, we believe that a different approach is preferable.

In this section we shall consider how the depression affected people rather than how the depression created situations. Accordingly, we shall show what happened to those who lost their jobs, those who went hungry and became homeless, those who had money in the closed banks, those who marched to Washington in hope of winning a bonus, those who wandered from town to town, those who tilled the soil, and those who were fortunate enough to have jobs. Each of the chapters is an independent account that tells how the depression affected a particular group of Americans.

Because of this arrangement, the section lacks the continuity one expects to find in most books. It is suggested, therefore, that in order to keep in mind the chief milestones of the depression years, the reader should review the following list of dates:

1929

FALL Stock market crashes during October, signaling end of country's greatest speculative boom.

1930

WINTER Unemployment spreads as business activity contracts and workers are discharged.

SUMMER Drought strikes Midwest and Southern states.

FALL Many states receive aid from the American Red Cross.

WINTER Bank of the United States with sixty-two branches and four hundred thousand depositors in New York City is closed by the state.

President Hoover asks Congress to appropriate a hundred and fifty million dollars to aid the unemployed.

1931

WINTER Unemployment becomes worse. The current popular
song asks, "Brother, can you spare a dime?" The answer
usually is "No."

Shivering men and women are selling apples on street corners.

President Hoover leads a drive for money to help the American
Red Cross administer relief to over two and a half million
people.

SPRING The number of bank closings increases.

SUMMER The drought continues and worsens.

FALL Many social service agencies are running out of money
and are unable to help the unemployed.

1932

WINTER Congress establishes the Reconstruction Finance Corporation to lend money to banks, business, cities, and states
in order to stimulate business activity.

Four killed as three thousand riot outside Ford Motor Company
plant in Dearborn, Michigan.

Norris-LaGuardia Act limits granting of injunctions against
labor and outlaws "yellow dog" contracts.

SPRING More than ten thousand veterans of World War I march
to Washington, D. C., to demand a bonus.

SUMMER The number of farm failures increases.

Representatives of farm organizations meet in Washington,
D. C., to seek a program that can deal with the farm surplus
problem.

FALL Members of the National Farm Holiday Association block
roads leading to several Midwestern cities, hoping to force
farm prices higher.

Franklin Delano Roosevelt running on the Democratic ticket
defeats Herbert Hoover for the Presidency.

1933

WINTER Banks continue to fail. Michigan declares a bank holiday
and other states follow.

President Roosevelt inaugurated March 4. One of his first
official acts is to close all banks for a week.

SPRING Famous "Hundred Days" of the New Deal produce many laws designed to feed the hungry, aid the economy, help farmers and workers, and achieve social reforms.

SUMMER Stock market breaks again, many stocks slipping 5–20 points.

NRA and the Blue Eagle (that bring regulation of prices and wages) are introduced with parades in many cities.

FALL Business activities gradually picking up; public works projects give employment to more and more men and women who were on the dole; relief made available to all who are in need.

1934

SPRING Serious drought in Midwest destroys winter wheat and causes bad dust storms.

SUMMER General strike in San Francisco threatens famine, as all unions go out on strike in sympathy with longshoremen and marine workers.

FALL Half a million workers strike in the textile industry, over twenty killed in clashes between strikers and National Guardsmen. At request of President Roosevelt, strikers return to jobs while special committee investigates grievances, but no improvements in wages or working conditions are realized.

1935

WINTER Works relief bill amounting to $4,880,000,000 is passed by Congress.

SPRING Supreme Court declares the NRA unconstitutional on "Black Monday," May 25.

SUMMER Congress passes the Wagner Act, cornerstone of the New Deal labor policy. Social Security Act also becomes law.

FALL The Federal dole (direct relief) terminated at a cost of $3,694,000 since it was instituted in May, 1933.

1936

WINTER The Federal act creating job-insurance goes into effect.

The Agricultural Adjustment Act is declared unconstitutional by the Supreme Court.

FALL Franklin Delano Roosevelt is reelected for second term.

WINTER The new Congress of Industrial Unions (CIO) starts campaign to include automobile workers within its ranks by halting work at three General Motors plants.

1937

The Supreme Court upholds constitutionality of the Wagner Act and the Social Security Act.

Major strikes caused by the Wagner Act in automobile and steel industries are settled.

1938

The stock market sags again and business activity falls.

The second Agricultural Adjustment Act becomes law.

"Pump Priming" is the term used to describe additional millions of dollars spent on public works and other projects in order to get the economy moving again.

1939–1941

The gradual rise in war production due to the European conflict and the resulting improvement in the nation's economy help to erase the scars of the depression.

On December 7, 1941, the day Pearl Harbor is attacked, the nation is plunged into war and into a wartime prosperity that is the reverse of the depression economy of the nineteen-thirties.

4

"NO ONE HAS STARVED"

The Hunger Years

"No one has starved," President Hoover asserted several times. He was repeating what he had been told, and pointed to the decline in the death rate to prove it. Unfortunately, this was not true.

According to reports received late in 1930 by the contemporary magazine, *The Survey*, a periodical devoted to the field of social service:

IN ST. PAUL "They give relief in the form of grocery and coal orders and two days' work a week on public improvements."

IN NEW YORK "The Sisters of St. Vincent's Hospital give

bread and a cup of soup to whoever comes to their door, but the numbers have mounted to hundreds and the Sisters fear that they cannot continue to feed them."

IN DETROIT "Some 100,000 people were hard hit and of these 20,000 were hungry."

IN PHILADELPHIA "The Committee of One Hundred on Unemployment—extended itself to a membership of 400 —geared up machinery to meet the needs of 125,000 men and women without employment and at the end of their resources."

IN 23 MEDIUM-SIZE CITIES "The number of families helped increased 146 per cent between August, 1929, and August, 1930. Private relief agencies frankly admit their lack of resources to cope alone with the situation."

Statistics mean nothing until we look behind them and seek out the actual people who make them up. Here is what happened to some families who made the statistics:

In New Orleans the Montery children picked up scraps of meat and vegetables that were cast aside at the market.

The Bertleys of Atlanta ate two meals a day, consisting of corn bread, salt meat, and dried beans. Mrs. Bertley suffered fainting spells which the doctor said were caused by lack of food.

The Giamios of Madison fed their children potatoes and bread with beans for meat.

Mrs. Cardini of New York City said, "We eat little— that's what we do."

The day before Christmas, 1931, a constable found a young couple starving in Sullivan County, New York. They had been without food for three days and the wife was unable to walk.

During the winter of 1932 New York City hospitals admitted ninety-five people suffering from starvation; twenty of them died. Another 143 men, women, and children became victims of malnutrition and of this number twenty-five did not survive. These figures do not include those who either were not admitted to hospitals or succumbed from other diseases caused by starvation.

In September, 1932, police found a woman, thirty-three, and her small daughter sleeping outdoors under a strip of canvas near Danbury, Connecticut. They had been living for the past five days on apples and wild berries.

The following summer, 1933, former President Hoover went fishing in the Rocky Mountains. One morning a man awakened him suddenly and led him to a shack where a child had just died of starvation. Seven others were almost dead from lack of food. Mr. Hoover took the children to the nearest hospital and raised over three thousand dollars to help care for them.

The cases are almost endless. Today it is difficult to imagine how people could be without food. Somehow during the depression most of the unemployed managed to keep their families alive on substarvation diets. Many did it by starving themselves to the danger point so that their children could eat. Some even left the house during mealtimes lest they take more than their share. This is how a few of the unemployed in Philadelphia managed when their meager relief checks were cut off.

THE BRAVE PEOPLE OF PHILADELPHIA

Mrs. Pauline Taylor opened the envelope from the Philadelphia social service agency. With her usual weekly check of $4.23 there was a brief printed notice. When the short bent widow had read it she slowly collapsed on the stoop and held her head in her hands.

This would be the last check. It was dated April 11, 1932. The agency had run out of money. There was not even enough cash left to send her and the other families one more allotment of $4.23, all that was keeping her and the three children from starvation. The small ones were always hungry, and Mrs. Taylor did her best to get by on as little food as possible. It was bad enough feeding the four of them on sixty cents a day, and this left no money for rent, clothing, or the many other things they needed. Now there would not be a penny coming in until the city could obtain funds from the Federal government.

"Children," she called, after she had struggled back upstairs, "we're really going to have to tighten our belts. From now on it's two meals a day." Meals, she thought to herself, if that is what you could call them. "We'll eat breakfast at eleven and supper at five," she added.

"What will it be, Mom?" Kevin asked. Kevin was even thinner than the others.

"Don't know yet," Mrs. Taylor said. She had half-figured out their daily menu but did not have the heart to tell the children. Breakfast would be cocoa, bread, and butter. Supper would be a can of soup.

The Taylors ate better than their neighbors, the Fishers, who during the next two weeks were twice without food for a day and a half. Mrs. Fisher walked up and down the docks looking for vegetables that might have fallen off passing farm wagons. Occasionally a fish dealer would feel sorry for her and give her an unsold flounder at the end of the day.

For the Parkinsons meals consisted of potatoes, rice,

bread, and coffee. No fats, no proteins, no fresh green vegetables or milk. But they were better off than the Frankels, who ate nothing for two days except bread and then splurged on bread and coffee for breakfast and bread and carrots for dinner. Compared to the McCools, the Frankels were fortunate. The McCools lived for eleven days on potatoes while the Renzeris existed on dandelion greens that Mr. Renzeri gathered in the fields.

On April 22, public funds became available and once more grants of $4.23 per family were mailed to those on relief. Of this money $3.93 was supposed to be for food, the rest for other necessities of life. Now recipients of these checks could live again like kings and queens!

The citizens of every city were not as fortunate as those who lived in Philadelphia. Chicago, which was one of the cities hardest hit by the depression, was bankrupt and existed on tax anticipation warrants which the bankers reluctantly cashed for a time. The Windy City had one of the worst reputations for helping its unemployed and needy citizens, the children suffering along with the adults.

THE CRISIS IN CHICAGO

"For God's sake, help us feed these children during the summer," was the plea of Chicago's School Superintendent William J. Bogan to the secretary of the governor's relief committee early in June, 1931. He had found that many principals and teachers were spending their own money to provide free nourishing lunches for hungry schoolchildren.

Shortly thereafter, the teacher of a third grade unlocked her classroom one morning and settled wearily into her chair.

"What's the matter, Miss Winston?" an arriving pupil asked. "Stay up too late listening to the radio?"

"Yes, yes, I guess that's it," Miss Winston said, attempting to smile. There was no sense telling the small child she had been awake all night, her mind tortured with worry for the dozen or more children in her class who were becoming more and more undernourished. They were listless now, uninterested in their work, unable to concentrate for any period of time. She suspected that their free lunch was the only meal they ate. What would happen to them and the eleven thousand other hungry children when school closed for the summer?

She put off speaking about it until just before dismissal.

"Girls and boys"—her voice sounded unnatural—"I— I wonder if any of you can ask your parents for money to help us to buy food for the children whose fathers are out of work? You know we have been giving them lunch but we are running out of money." She paused and looked about the class anxiously. "How many will ask?"

A half-dozen hands went up. Then Elliott, the brightest boy in the group, waved his right arm vigorously.

"Yes?"

"Miss Winston, my dad read in the newspapers that the teachers were paying for the lunches. Why do you need more money?"

Miss Winston had a certain kind of old-fashioned pride. She did not want these small children to know, but now she had to tell them.

"Well, Elliott, you see we can't do it any more." She avoided the children's eyes. "The city has run out of money. We teachers haven't received any salary for months ourselves. We're really unemployed, too."

The Hunger Riots

TROUBLE IN OKLAHOMA CITY

"We're hungry!"

"Let us in!"

"Our children are starving!"

"We can't find jobs."

The crowd of some five hundred unemployed men and women stood shivering in front of the grocery store not far from the center of Oklahoma City that afternoon of January 20, 1931. They were growing restive and unreasonable as they demanded food from the store. A delegation had just called on City Manager C. R. Fry, insisting that he furnish immediate relief, and then the crowd had marched up the street to stop at this store.

In vain Mr. H. A. Shaw, manager of the grocery, tried to quiet the crowd and urge them to move on.

"It's too late to bargain with us," a burly leader of the mob yelled, as he led the way into the store. Part of the crowd squeezed in behind him and proceeded to smash the interior of the building as they tossed canned goods off shelves and grabbed all the food they could carry.

Within minutes, emergency police squads arrived and used tear gas to disperse the people waiting their turn to enter the store. Soon the plate-glass windows cracked and broke as the looters tried to escape. Twenty-six were arrested and taken to the city jail.

Four days later, several hundred unemployed forced their way into a grocery and meat store in Minneapolis to help themselves to canned goods, fruit, bacon, ham, and other meats. When the owner of the store threatened to shoot at the crowd, someone grabbed the gun and broke his arm.

At the same time, another desperate group in the Twin City of St. Paul met to discuss the unemployment situation. Determined to get some extra food and luxuries for themselves, the men and women stormed into George Baglio's small store near the downtown area and stole over fifty dollars' worth of candy, apples, cigars, and cigarettes before police arrived.

Hunger riots and hunger marches were numerous and often Communist-inspired. During December, 1931, about fifteen hundred hunger marchers converged on Washington, D. C., from several cities. They sang Communist songs, tried without success to enter the White House and the Capitol, and then returned to their homes.

Perhaps the most futile demonstration took place on March 7, 1932, a day when the temperature hovered around zero. The jobless men who gathered in downtown Detroit had difficulty keeping their undernourished bodies warm. No wonder they welcomed a chance to do something different—anything that would help them forget their misery and perhaps hold the promise of jobs.

THE DETROIT HUNGER MARCH

By two o'clock, about thirteen hundred shivering men had gathered at Fort Street and Oakland Boulevard, a point within the city limits about two miles from the Ford River Rouge Plant at Dearborn, Michigan. The night before, William Z. Foster, head of the Communist Party, had addressed a mass meeting of some seven thousand workers at Detroit's Danceland. He urged everyone to join the next day the march to the Ford plant, where a delegation planned to present a request to Mr. Ford asking him to rehire the men he had laid off. Some fifty thousand men and women in Detroit were unemployed; a third of them had worked for the Ford Motor Company. One reason that Detroit had such a problem providing unemployment relief was that the Ford factory was outside the city limits. Hence, the company paid no taxes to help meet the Motor City's monthly relief bill of two million dollars.

As the marchers gathered, a few of the men distributed banners and placards, some of which read:

COME ON, WORKERS, DON'T BE AFRAID!
TAX THE RICH AND FEED THE POOR!
OPEN ROOMS OF THE Y'S FOR THE HOMELESS YOUTH!
WE WANT BREAD, NOT CRUMBS!
WE WANT JOBS

At a signal from their leaders, the crowd began to move toward Dearborn. As they marched they were joined by others who piled out of streetcars, automobiles, and even rented trucks. The men were in a good mood in spite of the fact that they would rather have been working than marching in subfreezing weather. The Unemployed Council of Detroit, a Communist organization which sponsored the hunger march, had obtained a police permit and Detroit policemen escorted the marchers as far as the city line where Dearborn police, headed by Acting Chief of Police Charles W. Slamer, barred the way. Chief Slamer asked if they had a marching permit.

"We don't need one," someone shouted.

"Come on, boys, let's go," another marcher called, and the crowd surged forward.

Immediately the Dearborn police discharged tear gas. It stopped the men in the front lines, but those farther back picked up rocks, bricks, and hunks of frozen mud and heaved them at the police. Then the wind blew the gas away, whereupon the crowd pushed ahead again only to meet another barrage of gas.

By this time, the men were on property of the Ford Motor Company. Those who received the second attack of the blinding gas tried to scatter, but soon faced another obstacle. From an overhead walk firemen shot streams of icy water at the crowd. Many managed to elude the frigid cascade by climbing up embankments.

Meanwhile, Harry Bennett, Ford's chief detective and "service man," had been talking with Governor Fred Green inside the factory. When told about the disturbance, he and Charles E. Sorenson, the general manager, dashed into a car and drove to the center of the trouble. Mr. Bennett wanted to tell the men that they would be rehired within two weeks when the new car models were ready for production.

As the Ford officials forced the car through the mob, Bennett was quickly recognized. Eager hands reached out to overturn the car, while others savagely hurled rocks at it. The occupants were rescued promptly by Ford police, who took the unconscious Bennett to the Ford hospital.

About this time the outnumbered Dearborn police, who had not yet drawn their guns, apparently panicked and fired point-blank into the crowd, killing four men. Instantly the unemployed workers began to scatter, defenseless against bullets. As soon as the Detroit policemen heard the shooting, they drew their revolvers and rushed into the middle of the melee. In a few minutes the police rounded up and arrested some sixty marchers, several of whom required hospital care. More than a hundred others were wounded, about half requiring hospitalization. A few of the marchers stayed behind to help friends and hailed cars on the highway to take the wounded home. Most cars refused to stop, and as they sped by the angry men pelted them with stones. This activity ceased as screaming sirens warned of the arrival of sheriff's deputies, heavily armed state troopers, and, later, troops from Fort Wayne, Indiana.

The following day, Prosecutor Harry S. Toy said that the riot was planned well in advance "by a small group of plotters or agitators." One of the dead was George Bassell, sixteen, who had been selected by the Communist Party to go to Russia in May to study Party training. Another was a Communist district organizer. Although the Communists had planned the march, there was no evidence that they had hoped to incite a riot. Nevertheless, they staged a gigantic funeral for the four martyrs.

Laid out in red coffins in Workers Hall, the dead were viewed by thousands who jammed into the building. Speeches took the place of prayers, and those who spoke swore to avenge their dead comrades by organizing the automobile workers into a union.

A crowd estimated at fifteen thousand followed the hearse to the cemetery. The usual signs were carried aloft. This time they read:

SLOW DOWN THE DAILY SPEED OF THE FORD PLANT
FORD GAVE BULLETS FOR BREAD

The funeral procession consisted of a hearse and other cars draped in red. Behind them marched numerous Communist organizations, each assembled behind its own banner. Hundreds of children wearing red berets with the hammer-and-sickle insigne followed. Finally came forty men bearing wreaths of red flowers. Many of the spectators who lined the streets wore red neckties, scarves, and bows.

At the cemetery twenty-eight musicians played "Communist hymns" and a dozen violins intoned a Russian funeral march. Then the four red coffins were lowered into a common grave and, as the crowd sang "The Internationale," the red flowers were tossed in, too. After a few speeches all went home as peacefully as they had come.

The next day 162 members of the Detroit police force joined the unemployed whom they had helped arrest. The city was so bankrupt it could not pay them. Shortly thereafter, Ford called the men back as production on the new model cars got under way. So ended the Detroit Hunger March. Four dead, scores wounded, nothing accomplished.

The American Brand of Philanthropy

The early colonists who settled this country frowned on poverty. Paupers were not respectable and the condition of being poor was thought to be the fault of an individual resulting from a character weakness. The authorities packed the poor into the almshouses along with the sick, the mentally disturbed, the blind, and the alcoholic. Those more fortunate paupers who were able to remain in their own homes received the traditionally meager "outdoor relief" which was in reality cash and food, a form of what we now call home relief.

"The presence in the community of certain persons living on public relief has the tendency to tempt others to sink to their degraded level."

This is not a contemporary statement but was made in 1884 by Mrs. Josephine Shaw Lowell, founder of the New York Charity Organization Society. The early social workers still believed that poverty was caused by a weakness of the individual who probably could be cured. Men were divided into two groups—idlers and workers. If one did too much for either of them, Mrs. Lowell held that there was danger a man would lose his desire to work. Fortunately, these ideas have changed, but society has not been able to abolish poverty.

Over the years, the almshouse gradually disappeared, but nothing took its place except homes for the aged. "Outdoor relief" became available in only a very few places. Since 1897, the indigent and needy of New York City, for example, have had to depend on private social service agencies for such help as they could afford to give. The same was true in many other communities, it being a time-honored belief that relief of the poor should be the obligation of charitable organizations rather than of the government.

During the early years of the depression, the cities appropriated small sums for relief, the politicians hoping that this would encourage the recipients to get jobs more quickly.

Actually, there was not enough money in most city treasuries to provide much aid. In one city, there was an increase of 300 per cent in the number of families aided but an increase of only 30 per cent in available funds. We have already noted that Chicago was bankrupt. Detroit was unable to collect taxes from property owners, who in turn could not collect rent from unemployed tenants. At one time, New York City employees contributed 1 per cent of their salaries to support a special fund so that the police could buy food for the starving.

The Reliefers

"Mr. John Williams, you're next," called the stout case worker in the hot and smelly relief office.

Mr. Williams, a handsome man in his late forties, walked briskly to the shabby desk. Although his clothes were worn, he was obviously a man who took pride in his appearance. He had delayed this visit as long as he could. Once prosperous, it had hurt his pride to realize that going on relief was the last resort.

"I'm Rose Barton," the case worker said, as she took a long form from the desk. "There are many questions we have to ask."

Mr. Williams nodded. A friend had told him how it would be. No detail would be overlooked; it would be almost as thorough as the questions they asked a prisoner. So this was what it was like to be poor!

"I am a civil engineer—or was. I worked until 1930 for a large company in the city, was laid off, found various selling jobs that didn't last, and haven't worked for the last thirteen months," he told Miss Barton, when she asked about his work experience.

"But I must have exact names, addresses, dates, duties, and salaries," she protested. "Then I must know about your personal finances."

His story was typical. There was a long period of unemployment and while he searched for a job first the savings account was exhausted. Next went the building-and-loan shares that were to put Joan and Ed through college. When that money was gone, they sold the car, pawned the jewelry and silver, and finally took the radio, the phonograph, a good rug, and the vacuum cleaner to a second-hand dealer.

"Have you any bank accounts?" Miss Barton asked.

"What are they?" Mr. Williams asked bitterly. "Of course not."

"And insurance policies? How much insurance do you have?"

"All I had has lapsed. Everything's gone except a policy for three hundred dollars."

"All right. You can keep that. You're allowed a 'funeral fund,' enough to bury you decently."

Half an hour later she had finished. "You'll hear from us after your case has been investigated."

"And meantime?

She shrugged. "You'll have to get along the best you can, as you have so far."

Two weeks later Mr. and Mrs. Williams were called to the relief office and told that the application had been approved. The case worker helped them work out a budget and instructed them on the use of the weekly food voucher and two dollars cash for their other expenses. Fortunately, there was no mortgage on the house, and although the taxes had not been paid for two years the city was not seizing property for delinquent taxes.

It was an odd experience that afternoon to shop as reliefers instead of cash customers. Referring to the printed lists of foods the Williamses selected only those items they could "buy" with the voucher. At last they took their selections to the clerk.

"Can't get those fresh beets," he said. "Only canned. Fresh aren't on your list."

"But they're cheaper than the canned right now," Mrs. Williams protested.

"Can't help that. And those eggs, they're not on the list this week."

In some ways life was quite different. The family's chief

concern was to make the food last from week to week, to conserve clothing, and to find free entertainment. The parents had to forget golf, tennis, and bridge. The children gave up swimming, ice skating, and other activities that required carfare to reach the athletic center. Movies, concerts, contributions to the church, an occasional ice-cream cone, even a newspaper were out of the question.

On the other hand, life was unchanged in many respects. Mr. Williams still spent mornings looking for work and afternoons in the library. His lunch was a five-cent candy bar or a peanut-butter sandwich brought from home. Mrs. Williams, who once had a maid, did all the housework as she had been doing for over a year. The children still went to school. There was little or no stigma in being on relief. The family continued to see their old friends and had no social contact with the other reliefers whom Mr. Williams met each week when he went down for his voucher and two dollars.

Even the weekly voucher and cash were too good to last forever. A few months after the Williamses went on relief the city ran out of funds and the office was closed.

Hunger and suffering had not been strangers to President Hoover since he headed the relief organization that fed and assisted the homeless and starving Belgian people following World War I. He believed firmly that man was his brother's keeper and that the Federal government "should not make direct charitable gifts" to the needy. Speaking on the radio in 1931, he reminded his listeners of their heritage:

> No governmental action, no economic plan or project can replace that God-imposed responsibility of the individual man and woman to their neighbors. That is a vital part of the very soul of the people. If we shall gain in

this spirit from this painful time, we shall have created a greater and more glorious America. The trial of it is here now. It is a trial of the heart and conscience, of individual men and women.

Voluntary giving in the form of donations to community chests for the various health and welfare organizations was the President's answer to the problem. To help support these private agencies, unusual fund-raising events were held from time to time, one of the more spectacular being the drive for money conducted by the Committee on Mobilization of Relief Resources of the President's Organization for Unemployment Relief.

"I Will Share"

"I never thought I'd be helping the unemployed by going to a movie!" a gray-haired woman observed to her friend as they stood in line outside a theater in St. Louis. It was almost midnight, and they were cold from waiting so long.

The line started to move, and as they neared the box office they passed a sign that read:

ALL PROCEEDS FROM THIS PERFORMANCE DURING
NATIONAL MOTION PICTURE WEEK TO GO TO THE
UNEMPLOYED RELIEF

Throughout the nation in some twenty thousand movie houses that held fifteen million seats, people were seeing an extra midnight show to help those on relief.

This was but one of the many activities Owen D. Young, Board Chairman of the General Electric Company, had planned. Named head of the Committee on Mobilization of Relief Resources of the President's Organization for Unemployment Relief, he was determined to raise enough money during October and November, 1931, to see the destitute through the winter. Before he had finished with the drive most Americans had heard about it. All advertising and publicity outlets had been placed at his disposal to advertise the fact that America had a depression and that millions of Americans needed assistance.

There were thirty-five thousand billboards that carried pictures and appeals.

Former President Coolidge wrote a letter to be read by radio announcers urging everyone to give what he felt America was worth to him.

J. P. Morgan, the famous financier, made a rare appearance on a radio network to plead for funds.

Movie Czar Will Hayes created National Motion Picture Week.

In each city, various affairs were held to raise money, but as usual New York outdid itself. In order to make sharing as pleasant and painless as possible, there was something for everyone. For example: Supper dances at smart hotels were scheduled for the wealthy, triple-header basketball games appealed to athletic fans, a water carnival was held for lovers of aquatic sports. The drive reached a climax when ten thousand people jammed into Madison Square Garden. They were described by The New York *Times* as a "martial assembly proclaiming war on poverty and need." To help them make this great proclamation, a number of famous men and women spoke, the tedium of their speeches being relieved by the music of eight bands and twenty-two glee clubs. During the same week some seventeen thousand hand-picked workers under the direction of two thousand committee officers scoured the city for coins and dollar bills not already contributed through one of the special events.

"STAMP OUT WANT"

"You mean we're supposed to ask people to give only a dime a week for twenty weeks?" The woman's worn clothing gave her the appearance of needing charity more than the poverty-stricken for whom she was going to solicit funds.

"Yes, but if a person can give more, by all means ask for it," the block chairman said.

"But what good is ten cents a week when we have thousands of people to feed? How many meals will a dime provide?"

Patiently the chairman explained that the goal of the nationwide drive was to get everyone who could afford it to give at least ten cents a week or a minimum of two dollars. This was another activity of the President's Organization for Unemployment Relief which hoped that the drive would raise enough money to help all the unemployed. Contributors would buy a stamp each week and paste it in a special folder.

"Another thing," the chairman said, "we want you to ring every doorbell on the block, even in apartments or homes of those who can't give. We must know of any people who are starving or in want."

It was a gigantic effort to make certain that every block had ten block aiders. In New York City alone, 38,316 men and women worked under 7,387 chairmen. Those who rang doorbells ranged in age from eight to eighty. Every profession and walk of life was represented as the army of callers went forth and collected more than $1,300,000.

In spite of these drives, and tens of thousands of other local appeals for money, it became increasingly difficult for social agencies to keep their doors open as more people applied for help. Most organizations had to abandon their normal activities and concentrate on giving families money for food, but the time came for most of them when the money stopped, as was the case in Philadelphia. With social agencies unable to help, with cities bankrupt, there was no place to turn except to the Federal government.

The Emergency Relief Act of 1932 permitted the Reconstruction Finance Corporation (RFC) to lend the states up to $300,000,000 for relief. By the end of the year the governors had borrowed only a tenth of that sum, which was inadequate in view of the tremendous need.

The Breakdown of Relief

As the short thin woman approached the official in the relief office, she wearily stood by her the child she had been holding. The line had moved quickly, encouraging her to believe that she would get help promptly. It was mid-April, 1932.

"We're out of food. My husband hasn't worked for a year," she told the man at the desk. Then she pointed to the small child. "This one here's always hungry, and there's three more home in bed. I keep 'em there as much as I can so they won't get such big appetites and—"

"I'm sorry, madam," the wooden voice interrupted. "We can't do anything for you."

Her eyes widened first in disbelief, then clouded with fright.

"What do you mean, you can't do anything?" her voice quavered slightly as it started to rise. "They told me at the agency to go see the relief. The lady said they didn't have any more money but you could help."

It was the same story the others had told him. Hundreds more would recite it each succeeding day.

"I'm sorry, madam. The city has temporarily run out of money, too. Maybe some private agency can help you. Since April 9th we've been turning down seven hundred families a day."

"I don't care about them! I have four kids to feed and I got to get help." She was becoming hysterical and the policeman stationed nearby shook his head sadly as he started toward her. "Don't tell me New York's too broke to help me. I won't leave until—"

"Lady, you heard what he said." The officer gently took her arm to ease her out of the office.

The situation was just as bad, if not worse, in other cities across the United States.

A short time later, the editors of *The Survey* studied thirty-seven cities and reported that

> without plans, without strong national leadership, with meager and uncertain funds, these cities have some way, somehow muddled through the winter, keeping their people alive, but at what cost of broken spirit and human suffering, only God knows.
>
> Complete breakdown is imminent. The fallacy of the idea that private funds could cope with a situation of such proportions as this one is remorselessly exposed. Private funds have been little more than a thin emollient on a deep wound.
>
> More distressing than the evidence of past muddling is the lack of evidence of any real statesmanship for the

future. No rational adult can be blind to what lies ahead. The summer will bring little surcease in human need. Next winter will be worse, not better.

Yet Congress is deaf, legislatures are adjourning, cities and counties are temporizing with pinchbeck appropriations, and private social agencies are in positions they cannot sustain. There is no evidence of any real facing of what is on the doorstep, or let alone any preparation to deal with it.

Nobody Is Going to Starve

It was little wonder that the nation's hungry looked to a new Congress and a new administration for help. Nor did the New Deal let them down. In contrast to President Hoover's assertions that no one had starved, the new President promised that "nobody is going to starve." Congress backed him up two months after the inauguration with the Federal Emergency Relief Act, which shifted to the Federal government the burden of providing relief to bankrupt or hard-pressed communities. It provided the Federal Emergency Relief Administration with half a billion dollars for direct relief to be dispensed to the states.

Much as cash relief was needed, the real answer to the problem was a job for every able-bodied man and woman. How the New Deal tackled the problem of unemployment is told in the next chapter.

5

PROSPERITY IS JUST
AROUND THE CORNER

The Last Hope

It was still dark, and an icy December wind was blowing across Manhattan into the Bronx. The church clock struck five as Alex McNair, a thin nineteen-year-old, locked the door behind him and pushed his way up the street against the gale. He wore a ragged sweater, faded bluejeans, and sneakers. Behind in the cold flat he left his mother and younger sister. Since his father had died Alex had become the breadwinner, only there were no jobs with which to win bread. Too proud to apply for charity, the McNairs had managed somehow by selling most of their possessions, until now there was nothing to eat and no money to pay the long-overdue rent.

It was only yesterday that despair had unexpectedly turned to hope when someone told Alex where he could get a job; not much, three days a week, but it was work and it paid fifteen dollars.

"Don't worry, Mom," he reassured her, "everything's going to come out all right. With fifteen dollars every week we'll be on easy street." It was the first time he remembered seeing her smile in more than a year.

Now he hurried along the dark streets until he came to the end of the line where men were standing, waiting, four abreast.

"How much farther does it go?" Alex asked an elderly man whose sad eyes looked out from a wrinkled face.

"Down to the corner and two blocks to the office."

"But it's only ten after five and I thought I'd be first!" The boy's voice was bitter. "There'll never be enough jobs by the time we get there." He rubbed his arms and stamped his feet to keep warm.

"Don't give up yet. Wait and see," the old man advised.

At six-thirty a policeman came on duty and slowly patroled alongside the queue. He was not needed. The men would have taken care of anyone who had tried to crash the line or slip into a better position.

By seven o'clock a few workmen carrying their lunch pails walked along the other side of the street, their eyes self-consciously avoiding the men. Suddenly Alex began to shiver violently. So cold and hungry that he lost control of himself, he began to sob and shake. This was a familiar sight to those about him. Quickly a space opened, sympathetic hands moved the boy into it and then the men pressed close to him. Soon the warmth of their bodies and the reassuring voice of an old man restored circulation and calm.

Seven-thirty, and a short man dressed in an old ulster

and a bowler hat walked slowly along the line, expertly estimating its size.

"That's him!" whispered the old man. "It's Mr. Matthews."

"Yes! That's the boss!" another said.

Some sixteen years before, William H. Matthews, who was with the Association for Improving the Condition of the Poor, believed in giving the unemployed jobs rather than a handout. Initially, he provided six men with rakes and shovels and put them to work in the Bronx Botanical Gardens, paying them with funds from his department's budget.

Since that time his method of helping those out of work had become widespread, for it saved families from the stigma of public charity or the breadline. During the early days of the depression his work projects were often the only hope unemployed heads of families had of finding a job in New York City. His employees went throughout the five boroughs working in parks, repairing public buildings, cleaning churches and schools, or doing any job that would keep them busy and make them feel that they were accomplishing something worthwhile. During the month of May, 1930, Mr. Matthews had employed 730 men and paid them $46,790 in wages at the rate of fifteen dollars a week for a three-day week. Soon there were thousands who needed work, many more than he could ever hope to use. Something had to be done, for every day the line of men that led to his door grew longer.

After spending each morning supervising the hiring, Mr. Matthews devoted the rest of the day, and often the evening, to raising funds. An able and persuasive speaker, by December of 1930 he had raised over eight million dollars, having interested many millionaires and important financiers in the project.

His day started early because the unemployed were always there. This particular morning, as was his custom, he hooked the double doors back at eight o'clock, then faced the crowd.

"Two at a time, boys. Take it easy, now." Slowly the line started to move as the first men edged forward into the doorway, felt the blessed warmth, then climbed the stairs. Several minutes later, back where Alex waited, still shielded from the cold by his new friends, the men cheered as they saw those ahead advance.

"A cup of coffee would taste good right now," someone said.

"Yeah, and a doughnut, too," added another.

"Be noon before you get anything to eat, if you're lucky," a bass voice growled.

They moved a bit and stopped, took five steps, then waited five minutes before they went forward again.

It was eleven o'clock before Alex and his companions reached the door. Although the day was almost half gone, the boy reasoned that Mr. Matthews had jobs for them, otherwise he would have told them to go home. He could see the door, and a few minutes later he was inside. Now he didn't care how long it would take to get upstairs because he was warm for the first time in six hours. He even forgot his hunger.

Step by step they made their way slowly to the large room above. At the top of the stairs a man barred any further advance. Behind him men sat at writing desks, each filling out a required form. Again there was a long wait, then Alex's heart began to race. Mr. Matthews was coming toward them, a box of blue tickets in one hand. There were jobs, enough blue tickets for every man standing on the stairway!

"Sorry, men," Mr. Matthews said. It seemed to Alex as though he were looking only at him. "Jobs are all gone for the day." The crowd groaned. "There'll be more tomorrow and you'll be the first to get them. I'll give each of you a blue ticket and this will entitle you to a job."

Alex gulped. No job until tomorrow. What would they do in the meantime for food? How would they pay the rent and—

"Now move up here," Mr. Matthews was saying, "and walk by me, one at a time. Married men only, provided you're residents of the city."

Married men only! The words froze in Alex's brain. *Married men*—

"Here, son, step up." Mr. Matthews was nodding at him. Alex mechanically stepped forward. "You married, boy? You look too young."

"Yes, I mean no, sir." Alex was unable to think clearly. "I'm the only one in our family who can work. Please, sir, my dad's dead. There's Mom and Nancy and—we're all out of—"

"Sorry, son, a rule's a rule. Only married men. Now please step—"

"But we'll be thrown out on the street if I don't get money!"

"I'm sorry, son, but I can't do anything to help you. Next man."

Fighting to hold back the tears, the boy pushed his way downstairs and out onto the street. Chin sunk into his chest and hands thrust into his pockets, he leaned against a lamp post, too tired, disappointed and dejected to return home. Now he had no choice but to apply at one of the relief agencies for assistance.

"Buy Now for Prosperity"

Philip H. Gadsden, President of the Philadelphia Chamber of Commerce, did his best to produce jobs for the three million people like Alex who were out of work.

"Do you know that if every wage-earner in America would 'Buy Now' to the extent of fifteen cents a day," he announced, "it would release enough capital to employ ten million unemployed at $6.25 a day? A mere fifteen cents a day would put $2,184,000 back into circulation per year." Under his direction, the Philadelphia Chamber of Commerce launched a "Buy Now" campaign in November of 1930. A correspondent of the Washington *Star* told how it was done:

> The city woke up last Monday morning to find "Buy Now for Prosperity" placaded on all its streetcars, being blared at them over the radio, plastered on the bills they received in their morning mail, on the caps of the babies' milk bottles, drummed at them from the end of every motion picture in town, hurled at them from the store windows of every merchant in the city, shouted at them from the head of every luncheon-meeting table, glaring at them from every streetcar, subway and elevated seat, plastered all over every railroad station, blazing forth from the first page of every morning and afternoon newspaper in the city, spread all over every available signboard in the city —in short, put where every man, woman and child in the city would see it hundreds of times a day.

The slogan worked like a charm. People jammed the stores, money began to circulate, jobs seemed more numerous. Immediately the movement spread throughout the country, and the Lions International aided the campaign with the promise that each of its eighty-five thousand members would spend a hundred dollars in one week and get five friends to do the same, thus putting two million dollars in circulation, "enough money to swing the depression from its rut."

Confidently the Chicago *Daily News* proclaimed that "the 'Buy Now' campaign rests on a sound business principle . . . the worst of the business slump is over and the upward trend is unmistakable."

Experience failed to bear out this optimistic assertion. Governor Eugene R. Black of the Atlanta Federal Reserve Board warned that the campaign was doomed to failure because the average citizen had only a limited amount of money to spend and if he went on a shopping spree there would have to be a period of recuperation before he could start buying again.

"What is needed is sustained purchasing power," Governor Black pointed out, and eventually he was proved correct as the economic barometers kept falling and unemployment continued its steady rise.

The Apple Merchants

As the steam ran out of the "Buy Now" campaign, many of the unemployed went into business for themselves as apple merchants. The International Apple Shippers Association promoted the sale of surplus apples with the slogan *Buy an Apple a Day and Send the Depression Away!* Soon every street corner seemed to have its stand, an upturned wooden crate on top of which brightly polished apples were pyramided.

During November, 1930, in New York City alone, there were between five and six thousand stands at one time. Apples sold for five cents each and brought a profit of about three dollars for a crate of a hundred. A lucky apple seller in a good location, or one who worked late in the theater district, might occasionally make six dollars a day.

One man who got religion in a city mission received two dollars and a quarter so that he could go in business for himself. He bought a crate of apples for two dollars and pooled his remaining quarter with four fellow merchants for a cab to take them up to the heart of the city's business district.

"Most of my customers were dressed as poorly as I," he said later. "I think lots of them buy the apples to fill their stomachs, so they can skip a meal. Generally they start eating as soon as they get hold of the apple. Well-dressed people mostly hurry by as if they didn't want to look at you."

By midwinter, 1931, there were almost twenty thousand apple stands on the streets of New York City. After officials turned them from busy thoroughfares most of the stands disappeared. Perhaps a few of the proprietors joined the six thousand shoeshine boys and men who lined the sidewalks calling attention to every pair of unshined shoes that passed. Five cents bought an expert shine and an extra nickel was ample additional reward for the shiner, who seldom found enough customers to earn a decent living.

People would try anything to earn a dollar. In Colorado during 1932 the State Board of Vocational Training opened placer mining schools in more than twenty cities. Within the first six weeks more than eight thousand people took the eight-day course that taught them how to pan streams for gold. It was hard work, and the only fortune those hopeful men and women found was an average daily earning of between twenty-five and fifty cents.

Men Wanted

As the depression gained momentum, unemployment grew like a giant snowball rolling downhill slowly. From three million in April, 1930, the number of jobless soared to four million within six months and almost doubled during the next year. By October, 1932, eleven million were idle, and when Franklin D. Roosevelt took office in March, 1933, it was estimated that the total had risen to somewhere between twelve and fifteen million.

With the country's economy creaking along and hundreds of men competing for every job, wages sank to new depths. Department stores paid sales clerks as little as five dollars a week, factory workers vied for jobs that paid but twenty-five cents an hour or even less. Ten dollars a week could get a fine secretary and ten dollars a month a servant. Hundreds of men would line up whenever a notice was posted regarding a job opening. Even the prospect of a few low-paid hospital positions would create a queue extending around the block.

It was always the same for those who went hopefully from one personnel manager to the next. The man would look down at his desk and finger some papers.

"Sorry, but we're not hiring anyone right now." Then he would look up, smile slightly and add, "But come back next year. We probably can use you then." Next year was a long time off, especially for the head of a family who had spent his savings.

When he turned to the help-wanted advertisements placed by the various employment agencies in the metropolitan dailies, it could be even worse.

The ads are still preserved in the rag editions or microfilm copies of any big city newspaper. The casual reader would think that no able-bodied man who really wanted to work during the depression needed to apply for a dole. Take February, 1933, for example, when over twelve million were unable to find jobs. Here are some of the listings that appeared in the advertisement of just one New York City employment agency:

Traveling Auditor, $3,600
Credit Manager, Open
Buyer Men's Clothing, $3,600
Salesman, Baking Exp., $3,100
Salesman, fruits, jars, Ohio, $3,000
Advertising Manager, $2,600
Office Boy, H. S. Grad., $15
Boys 14-15, 1 yr. H.S., $12

Too often, unfortunately, these jobs never existed at all.

"Sorry, that job's just been filled," the interviewer in the employment agency would say, or he might send you to an employer. There it would be the same story, but the personnel manager might congratulate you on your good fortune because you are qualified for a sales position which had miraculously just opened.

"I'm afraid we can't afford to pay you a salary, but the commissions are very liberal," he would assure you. You shake your head wearily, get to your feet and leave. You could tell him that the newspapers were full of help-wanted advertisements for salesmen, all promising liberal commissions and excellent futures. The only catch was that during a depression nobody buys. You could also tell him that now you know the advertisement for an accountant was just a cruel come-on—but what's the use?

The meanest deception of all was the practice of unscrupulous employment agencies that demanded their fee in advance. The applicant was assured of a job, then told that if he reported to the company he would definitely be hired but he must first pay the agency its fee, a week's salary, in advance. After the grateful aspirant had paid the fee, he went to claim the job but was rejected for lack of proper qualifications. When he returned to the employment agency the man who interviewed him was too busy to see him again and refused to refund his money.

The Reconstruction Finance Corporation

There were not likely to be many openings even at the bona fide employment agencies until something was done to create a need for workers throughout the country. As early as 1931, the United States Chamber of Commerce had proposed a plan to lick the depression by creating a national organization of businessmen and industrialists who would work closely with trade associations and control production, stabilize wages, and fix prices as required. Such action would mean repeal or temporary exemption from the antitrust laws, but businessmen were hesitant to permit the government to become involved in such a project.

To create new jobs, the President asked Congress to approve the establishment of the Reconstruction Finance Corporation (RFC), which would lend money to industry and those states in need of financial assistance. The governors in turn were to take the funds and initiate public works projects. This, Mr. Hoover hoped, would start the wheels of industry spinning again and assure the return of prosperity and full employment.

The RFC did not have enough money to do the job. The cash helped save some banks, railroads, and other businesses. It provided salaries for Chicago's unpaid teachers and it made loans to help finance New York State's Jones Beach, San Francisco's Oakland Bay Bridge, the Pennsylvania Turnpike, and other worthwhile projects. As the first program of Federal aid, it paved the way for the hundreds of agencies which were to come later under the New Deal.

It did not, however, make available sufficient spending to give the American people the purchasing power they needed to get the economy back to normal. Since the RFC failed to lick unemployment, economic conditions continued to worsen, and by the time of Franklin D. Roosevelt's inauguration on March 4, 1933, a crisis had developed.

Thousands of banks were closed, business failures were mounting rapidly, many cities were bankrupt, the relief system had long since broken down, a third of the labor force was out of work, many people were slowly dying of starvation. Young people, unable to find work, had created a national problem as they drifted aimlessly from city to city, riding freight cars, walking the roads, hitching rides, and begging food. For millions life had become an existence of despair without hope.

Saving the Nation

"This great Nation will endure as it has endured, will revive and prosper," the new President said defiantly.

After outlining the tasks that needed to be done, he

warned that if Congress did not do the job he would demand "broad Executive power to wage a war against the emergency, as great as the power that could be given to me if we were in fact invaded by a foreign foe."

A month later the Civilian Conservation Corps, with an initial grant of three hundred million dollars, began enrolling two hundred and fifty thousand youths between the ages of eighteen and twenty-five whose families were on relief. In addition to his bed and board, each man received thirty dollars a month, of which twenty-five dollars went to his family. Directed by the War Department, the CCC's, as they were called, worked on soil conservation, flood control, and reforestation projects.

On May 12th, Congress approved the Federal Emergency Relief Act with an appropriation of five hundred million dollars, half to go to destitute states and half to other states on the basis of matching each Federal dollar with three to be spent by cities and states. Recognizing that these were only stop-gap measures, Congress next approved the National Industrial Recovery Act which provided, among other things, for a Public Works Administration with a budget of three billion, three hundred million dollars.

After approving this act, President Roosevelt said:

"The law I have just signed was passed to put people back to work, to let them buy more of the products of farms and factories and start our business at a living rate again. This task is in two stages: first, to get many hundreds of thousands of the unemployed back on the payroll by snowfall, and second, to plan for a better future for the longer pull. While we shall not neglect the second, the first stage is an emergency job. It has the right of way.

"The second part of the [National Recovery] act gives

employment by a vast program of public works. Our studies show that we should be able to hire many men at once and to step up to about a million new jobs by October 1 and a much greater number later.

"We have worked out our plans for action. Some of it will start tomorrow. I am making available $400,000,000 for state roads under regulations which I have just signed and I am told the states will get this work under way at once. I have also just released over $200,000,000 for the Navy to start building ships under the London Treaty."

At last someone had proposed a bold plan to fight the depression, and countless thousands of Americans took hope. There was further cheer as the Public Works Administration with its budget of $3,300,000,000 started construction of hospitals, college buildings, highways, public buildings, and various municipal projects. Construction workers who had been idled by an almost complete absence of building found their services once again in demand. Architects, engineers, and office workers were hired to plan and administer the projects. Factories received new orders as manufacturing production almost doubled in July over March. For a few months there was a minor business boom, but it quickly died because red tape and bureaucrats slowed the PWA to a point where it lost much of its usefulness.

The Civil Works Administration

Again millions of families looked forward to another winter without work. At this point Harry Hopkins, a member of the New Deal family, persuaded the President to undertake a vast program of direct work relief, and another new agency, the Civil Works Administration, was established with $400,000,000 from PWA funds. Within a month the CWA was under way, and during the winter of 1934 provided income for some four million men and their families.

Like every hastily conceived project of such magnitude, there was bound to be confusion, waste, and political corruption. Only the registered unemployed and the needy were to be hired by the CWA, but when work tickets were printed and ready for distribution, the ward heelers and politicians grabbed many and gave them to their friends. In some cases, even policemen received tickets and distributed them to favorites on their beats.

In San Francisco Al Parsons, who was on relief, reported that on December 1, 1933, he was in a municipal hall when a short man came in with a box full of tickets. He told the unemployed who jammed the huge room to form a line, but there was a wild fight as the crowd surged forward in a free-for-all to grab the tickets, as it became obvious that only half of the two thousand jobless men would receive the pasteboards. Parsons managed to emerge with three quarters of a cardboard, which was honored after some fast talking. He was told to report to an empty lot that was to be transformed into a children's playground.

There, with several hundreds of other men, he spent six hours waiting and passing the time playing cards, an enterprise for which each man was paid $3.60. It was the same story the next day, for there were no tools. The rest of the week the CWA workers carried dirt in small wooden boxes and tried to dig holes with axes. Later, shovels and wheelbarrows arrived, but before the crew completed the project it was abandoned and the men were instructed to report elsewhere.

Thanks to many scandals, the insistence of conservative Democrats, and the accusations of Republicans that the program was inexcusably wasteful, Roosevelt discontinued it in the spring of 1934 and relief again became the responsibility of the Federal Emergency Relief Administration.

The Blue Eagle

Meanwhile, during the first part of September, 1933, in an effort to get the wheels of industry spinning again, parades were held throughout the nation to celebrate the advent of the NRA, or National Recovery Administration, and the Blue Eagle recovery program under the direction of General Hugh Johnson. The NRA (which was provided for in Title I of the National Industrial Recovery Act) was an experiment in a planned economy, the outgrowth of the earlier proposals of the United States Chamber of Commerce for regulating business. The intent of the NRA was to end cut-throat competition, raise prices and profits by cutting production, increase wages, and give labor a reasonable work week. Each branch of business and industry had its own committee representing business, labor, and the public, and was to adopt a fair code. As soon as each company covered by a code had complied with regulations, it was permitted to display the NRA emblem, a blue eagle.

Limiting production and eliminating competition was not the way to make business prosperous. Instead of helping to stimulate recovery, the NRA merely postponed it. What business needed was investment capital, and increased, rather than decreased, production. Little wonder that industrialists sabotaged the NRA and eventually the Supreme Court declared unconstitutional that part of the National Recovery Act which provided for the NRA

People like Steve Haballa of Harrisburg, Pennsylvania, began to wonder whether the New Deal had failed after the NRA had received its death sentence. Following four years of unemployment and poverty, Steve could see no prospect of ever returning to a steady job.

THE ORDEAL OF STEVE HABALLA

On November 2, 1931, Steve Haballa received his regular paycheck.

"You're done, Steve," the boss said. "Don't bother coming in Monday. We'll get in touch with you when we need you."

Steve looked at the man in amazement. For some time he had supervised the company's gangs of stonemasons and concrete workers, and had always been a faithful employee. Could it be true that he was being laid off after eighteen years with the Central Construction Corporation?

"Sorry, but there's no building going on here in Harrisburg," the boss added. "You know we haven't been busy. Good luck."

That evening Steve reviewed his situation. He had four children, a mortgage on his seven-room brick house, and not a cent in the bank. His only asset was a pair of family insurance policies with cash values totaling five hundred dollars. Nevertheless, he resolved to manage somehow without going to the relief agency and having to ask for help.

Within a short time the insurance policies had been cashed and he was forced to take out a personal loan of $120. During the winter of 1932 another construction company hired him, but the job ended after two weeks. Occasionally he found a day's work, and, because his credit was good, he was able to charge groceries at the small store down the block.

A year after losing his job Steve had no alternative but to go to a private welfare agency and seek assistance. Once the case worker had visited the family, asked numerous questions, and probed into the details of their finances, Steve became eligible for a five-dollar weekly food order. In addition, he received some Red Cross flour and each month the agency paid his fuel and electricity bills. Instead of the goulash and other tasty Hungarian dishes which Mary Haballa formerly had prepared for her family, they learned to like inexpensive foods like corn-meal mush, potatoes, sauerkraut, corned beef and cabbage.

In December of 1932 Steve went off relief when his old employer offered him a temporary job at forty cents an hour, but within three weeks he was back at the relief office. This time, to his surprise, he was put to work clearing brush in Wildwood Park at two dollars a day. After working five days he broke out with a bad case of poison ivy and was forced to apply again for relief. To help supplement the five-dollar food order, Mary earned a dollar a week cleaning the Magyar Baptist Church.

In January of 1933, the Harrisburg Building and Loan Association threatened to evict the family from their home for failing to make payments on the mortgage until Steve persuaded a bank officer to let them stay on and pay twenty dollars a month rent. Later during the year he had a lucky break—he found a nine-week job that paid sixty cents an hour, or $24.75 a week. These regular earnings enabled him to pay the back interest on the mortgage and a grocery bill of $115. By September of 1933, the family was again receiving a five-dollar food order and two quarts of milk a week for the children, and they returned to the old diet of corn meal, bread, potatoes, and very little meat. Soon one of the children was found to be suffering from malnutrition, but Steve could not afford the food required to correct the child's nutrition deficiency.

By February of 1934, the Civil Works Administration had begun to operate in Harrisburg, and Steve went to work for the State Highway Department as a foreman on a grading project at twenty dollars a week. When this agency expired in July, he returned to relief, this time not to a private agency but to the local office of the State Emergency Relief Board, which was now receiving Federal assistance. Once again a visitor came to the house to ask the same prying questions and after making copious notes and filling in endless questionnaires issued the usual five-dollar food order. In November, the relief board put Steve on a temporary real-estate survey job, but it did not last long enough to enable him to save sufficiently to stave off eviction.

On Christmas Eve the Building and Loan Association told Steve that he was being evicted for having paid only two months' rent in two years. Again he talked his way into staying on and in the middle of January obtained a job through the works division of the relief organization at $23.50 a week. At the end of the second week he was dismissed for having been absent for six days. By the time he was able to prove that he actually had worked every day, and the timekeeper admitted that he had made a mistake, it was too late to get the job back so Steve returned to the relief rolls.

Meanwhile, the gas had been turned off because the last relief check, made payable to the gas company, had been drawn for two cents more than the actual bill. The company refused to accept the overpayment, returned the check to the relief agency, and ordered the gas turned off for nonpayment of the bill.

In March, the bank finally evicted the family, and this time Steve was unable to talk his way back into the house. Instead, he borrowed $8.50 and paid two weeks' rent on a six-room apartment in a house that was stove heated and had neither hot water nor a bathroom. In July he was transferred to the direct relief rolls operated by the State Emergency Relief Board, which provided more generously than the private relief agency. The Haballa family now received weekly allotments as follows:

Food for six people	$ 7.75
Milk, one quart a day	.70
Clothing at the rate of 30¢ per week per person	1.80
Coal for kitchen range and heating house	2.50
Rent	1.40
Gas for cooking	.65
Electricity	.60
	$15.40

On October 22, 1935, Steve Haballa was transferred from direct relief to Works Projects Administration project No. 1991, where he became Case No. 4422-275, assigned to work on an underground passage being built at the State Insane Hospital. At last he could look forward to fairly steady employment, because the WPA, which had been created by the Emergency Relief Act of April, 1935, was destined to remain in operation until the depression was long past.

The Boondoggling Agency

At the outset the new agency established projects of extremely diverse types. Skilled women worked on sewing projects. Manual laborers were employed on road-building projects. White-collar workers and professionally trained men and women worked on educational, art, musical, theatrical, and even literary projects, but 78 per cent of the funds went for conservation and public construction.

The average monthly number of workers on WPA rolls from 1935 to 1941 was 2,112,000, with the peak employment of 3,238,000 coming in November, 1938. As the nation began to recover from the depression during 1935, 1936, and 1937, the number of unemployed dropped, and so did the WPA rolls. In the recession of 1938, the WPA projects helped take up some of the new unemployment, but with the return of prosperity in 1939 and 1940 the need for the WPA began to disappear and in 1941 it was voted out of existence.

At a time when there were only forty-three million jobs in the United States for the fifty-two million people who needed them, WPA helped take up some of the slack. Normal monthly turnover among those who were on the WPA rolls was 3 per cent, and the average man who joined WPA had to wait two and three-quarters years before he could leave and find a real job in private industry.

Working on "made" jobs was different from working on actual jobs in private industry, where the employer expected maximum efficiency in order to realize a profit. In the WPA bosses were easier on their men, hours were shorter, there was less real work to be done. Furthermore, there were usually more men on the rolls than necessary to accomplish the work since the ranks were padded to provide employment for the maximum number of workers on relief.

Because so many of the WPA projects were patently "made" work, the practice gave birth to a new word, *boondoggling.* Referring to the frequent use of this term, usually in a critical context, Roosevelt once said, "If we can boondoggle ourselves out of the depression, that word is going to be enshrined in the hearts of our people for years to come."

Apparently most people agreed with the President in spite of the general criticism. A survey conducted by *Fortune* magazine asked whether people thought direct cash benefits or jobs created by government provided better relief. It revealed that public opinion backed up the New Deal philosophy since only 9 per cent preferred cash payments against 74 per cent who favored jobs created by government.

In a report that was never published, General Hugh S. Johnson took sharp issue with this approach to helping the idle:

> Sixty per cent of this invented work is a needlessly expensive and fatuous gesture [he declared]. The only argument is that it preserves pride against the humiliation of home relief. Yet, to go on work relief, the rules (in New York) require that a man first go on home relief. To get there, he must submit to the equivalent of a pauper's oath. . . .
>
> The money should be disbursed as direct relief, except for worthwhile and necessary work on a basis of cost competitive with contemporary public construction.

During the six years that the WPA was in operation, it spent approximately $11,300,000,000 on some 250,000 projects. In spite of its faults, WPA provided the first continuous work relief program and substituted jobs for doles at a time when destitute men and women, many of whom had not worked for years, needed the psychological uplift of a job plus a steady, even though low, income.

Thus the WPA not only rehabilitated millions of Americans by providing active employment at a time when jobs were not available, it also helped build a reservoir of trained manpower which was needed soon thereafter when America became the "Arsenal of Democracy" during World War II.

6

THE MARCH ON WASHINGTON

It was a cold January day in 1932 and the air was thick with smoke as the Reverend James R. Cox, pastor of St. Patrick's Roman Catholic Church in Pittsburgh, stood on the church steps and looked down the street. As far as he could see there was a line of trucks and automobiles, each filled with men whom he had recruited for a trip to the nation's capital to ask Congress to do something about unemployment. Over a period of weeks Father Cox had collected money for food and gasoline, and now the moment was at hand. Ten thousand men had climbed into the thousand vehicles, ready to start what they felt was almost a holy crusade. They were orderly and quiet as the signal was given to the lead car and the procession picked up speed and moved out of Pittsburgh.

This was neither the first nor the last group of citizens to travel to Washington to present a petition to the Congress. In 1894, Jacob Sachler Coxey, who later became mayor of Massillon, Ohio, led an "army" of a hundred ragged men to the capital to get Congress to do something about hard times. Only a month before the Reverend Cox had assembled his "army," as previously noted, some sixteen hundred Red "hunger marchers" rode to the capital in trucks, tried unsuccessfully to force their way into the Senate, and then retreated as they sang "The Internationale."

As Father Cox's cavalcade rolled across Pennsylvania, a car loaded with medical supplies joined them. It was the gift of the people of Huntington, West Virginia. When the cars reached the tollhouse at Clarks Ferry Bridge over the Susquehanna River, tolls were neither offered nor demanded.

At Harrisburg, the men were welcomed by the Governor, who not only expressed his sympathy for their cause, but, more important, provided everyone with shelter for the night. At his request, state troopers and other law enforcement officials looked the other way whenever they spotted any of the group's vehicles, which still bore 1931 license plates.

It was ten-thirty the next night when Father Cox's lead car pulled into Washington. At his direction it stopped at a drugstore where he called the chief of police to tell him that his group had arrived. He and members of his staff then went to the Continental Hotel. A few of the men slept in the District National Guard Armory and the rest passed the night as best they could huddled in their cars or trucks to keep warm and dry.

In the morning, field kitchens rolled up from Fort Meyer and everyone became invited guests of the Army for a breakfast of apples, doughnuts, and hot coffee. When all had been fed, loudspeakers mounted on cars called:

"Attention! Attention! Fall in line, men, eight abreast and ready to march. Do it like gentlemen!"

Waving little American flags the men moved behind their band up to the steps of the Capitol, where Father Cox was greeted by Senator James John Davis and Representative Clyde Kelly of Pennsylvania. Gravely they received the formal petition for "the God-given right to work" and promised that it would be read to both houses of Congress that afternoon. Then, at a signal from Father Cox, the men swore allegiance to the flag and sang three songs.

Next, Father Cox went over to the White House and called on President Hoover. Here he presented a more detailed petition which called for a five-billion-dollar public works program, direct Federal appropriations for unemployment relief, help for farmers, and gift and inheritance tax increases to 70 per cent.

Mr. Hoover listened attentively, and with the comment that "We are giving this question our undivided attention," terminated the interview.

After laying a wreath on the tomb of the Unknown Soldier, Father Cox gave the order for the men to return to Pittsburgh. Soon the trucks and automobiles were on their way, but they left behind 276 stragglers who had wandered off to sight-see. Their train fare to Pittsburgh was paid for by one of Pennsylvania's most distinguished citizens, Secretary of the Treasury, Andrew Mellon.

Just what, if anything, Father Cox's "army" accomplished was never known. One result of the visit was surely never anticipated by either Father Cox or any of the ten thousand who participated in the demonstration. It came about some four months later when the newspa-

The utter dejection and loneliness of the unemployed during the Depression is typified by this penniless worker. *The Print and Picture Department, The Free Library of Philadelphia*

There was no place to go to look for work and the situation became hopeless as the years went on. *The Print and Picture Department, The Free Library of Philadelphia*

Families took to the road as in this scene in Georgia. Without automobiles many of them had to pull their possessions on makeshift wagons. *The Print and Picture Department, The Free Library of Philadelphia*

Faced with exhausted relief funds, Cleveland, Ohio, turned to the Federal Surplus Commodity Corporation for potatoes, cabbage and butter to eke out curtailed local food orders. Temporary distributing stations were established on streets and vacant lots to act as a stop-gap to prevent actual suffering until the state legislature could act on a more permanent solution of a relief problem that had been growing more acute in northern Ohio cities. This line extended for a block-and-a-half at one of the temporary distributing stations. *Acme*

pers carried a story about three hundred men who had hitchhiked their way from Oregon to St. Louis and then crossed the East St. Louis Free Bridge into Illinois. They were a pathetic group, dressed for the most part in old clothes, some wearing olive drab tunics, a few sporting overseas caps. Some carried pots in which they cooked their stews and coffee. A few had clubs, these men being designated "military police," to keep law and order.

The head of the Bonus Expeditionary Force, as the men called themselves, was Walter W. Waters, thirty-four, the former superintendent of a fruit cannery in Oregon. He was married, the father of two children, and had been unemployed for a year and a half when he decided to start the movement with the hope of forcing Congress to adopt the Patman Bill, which would provide immediate and full payment of a bonus by issuing $2,400,000,000 in paper money. Veterans had already received a bonus and many other benefits so that by 1932 expenditures for veterans already exceeded the combined veteran benefits paid by Great Britain, France and Germany.

The Bonus Expeditionary Force

During the middle of May, 1932, some three hundred former soldiers seized a Baltimore & Ohio freight train just outside East St. Louis, Illinois.

"Get off that train, you men," the railroad official shouted at the hijackers.

"Try and make us!" the veterans yelled, as they refused to leave. "Come and get us! We're going to Washington and we're taking this freight."

The railroad refused to move the cars and eventually the men reluctantly abandoned their perches, but they did not accept defeat. They immediately marched eight miles to Caseyville, where they lined up along the railroad track on a steep grade, after carefully soaping the rails. When a train consisting of thirty freight cars started up the hill, it soon stalled, whereupon someone cut the air hose and the men at once took possession of the rolling stock. While county and railroad police argued with Waters, ice in the refrigerator cars melted and food perished. After twenty-four hours the militia was called out, but trouble was averted when merchants from East St. Louis appeared with two hundred pounds of sausage meat in addition to other food, and free truck transportation was promised to Washington, Indiana.

Meanwhile, Brigadier General Pelham D. Glassford, Chief of Police for the District of Columbia, had been warned that the B.E.F. was coming, and he made preparations to billet the men in a vacant department store. They had hardly arrived on May 26th, however, before the General received an alarming report that ten thousand more veterans were on their way.

The marchers came, wave after wave of them, from every part of the country. They hitchiked, they walked, they stole rides in trucks, they climbed aboard empty freight trains. To men who were unemployed, discouraged, and tired of doing nothing, a trip to Washington that might win some extra money looked like a great adventure. Lack of cash to make such a journey was no obstacle. Hadn't the original B.E.F. boys received free food and transportation? These veterans knew that generous Americans would provide for them, too.

General Glassford, now responsible for dealing with all the marchers who had converged on Washington, told them that they could remain in the city no longer than forty-eight hours. When he made this pronouncement, the leaders laughed.

"We're staying until the bonus is paid," they told him.

As the men arrived they were assigned quarters in unused government buildings that were slated to be demolished. Army rolling kitchens were provided, bed sacks stuffed with straw were delivered from military warehouses, and local merchants donated food. The growing army quickly filled the vacant structures and a camp was then set up across the Potomac on the Anacostia flats. Here thousands of men, some with families, set up makeshift shelters using cardboard, orange crates, discarded mattresses, and other refuse gathered from the nearby dump. A fortunate few had borrowed pup tents from the Army, but many slept under the stars. When the wind blew, dust swirled; when it rained, the ground became a quagmire, and always there were swarms of flies and mosquitoes. Sanitary conditions were so deplorable that public-health officials feared an outbreak of typhoid.

General Glassford backed down from his original evacuation order to the B.E.F. by saying that as long as food and money held out the men might remain. In spite of the size of the army—some accounts say it grew to as many as twenty thousand—order was maintained at all times.

The Patman Bill was brought before the House for a vote and approved on June 15th. That night there was singing and rejoicing in the buildings occupied by veterans and on the Anacostia flats. All were certain they would win.

Two days later, the bill came to the Senate for a vote. While the lawmakers debated and voted, more than ten thousand men massed about the Capitol, waiting for the news. The city was tense. All officers' leaves had been canceled at the nearby fort. Officials were jittery and expected trouble. Then came the word—the Senate had tabled the bill! The bonus was dead. The veterans heard the news in bitter silence and returned slowly to their quarters. They had lost their fight; there was no hope for a bonus during this session of Congress as the congressmen now turned to other legislative matters.

Official Washington breathed easier, relieved to know that the crowd would now be leaving. The city was due for a surprise, though. Aside from a few men who packed up and started for home, the B.E.F. remained. A group continued to lobby for the bonus and newcomers replaced those who left. Residents of the District wondered what was going to happen next.

On June 21st, General Glassford persuaded the Pennsylvania and Baltimore and Ohio Railroads to take the men home at a cent a mile. Funds were lacking, however, and the plan failed. The army remained encamped.

A week passed and still nothing happened. Life on the Anacostia flats settled down to a routine and it seemed as though the B.E.F. was going to settle at Washington permanently. Another week slipped by, and finally on July 7th a worried Congress appropriated a hundred thousand dollars to help the men reach their homes. Each veteran could borrow as much as he required for the trip and the loan would be applied against the bonus still due him. The offer was good only to July 14th, and at first there was little interest. By July 10th, with only four more days left, 590 had applied for loans.

Meanwhile, a group of Communists led by John T. Pace had infiltrated the B.E.F. and through a campaign of vilification directed at Waters, deposed him and set up Pace as leader. Gradually events took a turn for the worse as the Communists stirred up trouble. Some of the veterans became more bold and bothersome as they strutted about the city. Residents grew fearful as police regulations were violated daily and men sprawled and slept on the lawns of the Capitol grounds. Government officials became apprehensive, for it was clearly evident that the B.E.F. was holding the capital in a state of siege and that the Administration appeared powerless to do anything about it.

On July 20th, more than a month after the bonus bill had been tabled, two hundred men marched on the White House but were driven back by tear gas. The next day General Glassford ordered the B.E.F. to vacate Washington by August 4th. President Hoover had instructed various government agencies to obtain the names of two thousand members of the B.E.F. and check government records to see how many were actually veterans. He learned that it was no longer necessary to humor these men, for only one third of them had ever served in the armies and many of the others were Communist or hoodlum elements. The fifty-odd men still living in the vacant government-owned buildings on Pennsylvania Avenue were told that the structures were to be razed and therefore they must be vacated immediately.

None of the invaders showed any signs of going home, and to make matters worse another seven hundred hungry ragged ex-soldiers from the Pacific Coast arrived with Roy Robertson in command. He was wearing his blue overseas cap and whipcord breeches. Behind his head was a steel brace from which heavy straps supported his chin. His spine had been badly injured while he was serving in the Navy.

On July 25th, there was more street fighting between police and B.E.F. members, who again tried to march to the White House. Three days later, as workmen started to demolish the buildings, the occupants were joined by a thousand men from the Anacostia camp who made an organized attack on the police and showered them with brickbats. In the confusion that followed, a policeman drew his revolver, killed two men, and wounded two more. Thereupon, General Glassford appealed to the District Commissioners to obtain help from the Federal government, since his men were outnumbered and no longer could maintain order in the city.

Something had to be done. It was clear that President Hoover must act. This was revolution, and such a rebellion could mushroom through the nation just as news of the original band of B.E.F. had triggered this crisis.

That afternoon, Secretary of War Patrick Jay Hurley, acting under instructions from the White House, ordered General Douglas MacArthur, Chief of Staff of the United States Army, to "surround the affected area and clear it without delay."

At 4:30 P.M., troops led by cavalry, followed by tanks, machine-gunners and infantry, rattled down Pennsylvania Avenue to the buildings which the men had refused to vacate. Tear gas quickly routed the more stubborn of the mob and the flat side of the saber drove them away from the capital, across the bridge to the camp at Anacostia, which was soon engulfed in flames and smoke. There were a few injuries but no deaths.

All that night and the next day pathetic groups of men could be seen on the roads leading from the city. Like discharged members of a defeated army, their bravado was gone, their spirit was broken. Once again they were their old selves, with nowhere to go but home and nothing to do when they got there. They would beg food, walk, steal rides, and eventually straggle ingloriously into their home towns.

When some of the marchers, including Waters, reached Johnstown, Pennsylvania, the mayor offered them asylum. Thanks to the generosity of unknown friends, all of these men received transportation home by train.

Thus ended the siege of Washington.

Twenty years later, John T. Pace testified before a Congressional committee that his Red bosses had ordered him to stir up riots.

"I was told to use every trick to bring about bloodshed in the hope that President Hoover would be forced to call out the Army. . . . I was told that Moscow had ordered riots and bloodshed in the hope that this might set off the revolution."

Moscow did not achieve its objective, but the method which the President reluctantly chose to rid the city of the B.E.F. undoubtedly helped to defeat him at the polls that fall.

7

THE BANKING CRISIS

When the Money Stopped in New Jersey

"Paul! Close your window and step outside. I have to tell you something."

"O.K., Burt."

Paul Anderson shut the small pane of glass, slid off the high stool, and let himself out of the barred cage, leaving a line of bewildered depositors in front of his window.

"Better get your money out before it's too late," Burt whispered. "One of the officers just warned me."

Paul looked about him anxiously as he nervously flexed his fingers. They were tired from counting out so many ones, twos, fives, tens, and twenties.

"Is—is it that bad? But why? I don't understand."

No one else understood, either. It was a few days before Christmas, 1930, and for the last two days long lines of men and women had queued in the bank's lobby as one depositor after another shoved withdrawl slips at Paul and the other tellers.

It was true that the big Bank of the United States in New York City had closed its doors a short time before, and that depositors had started a run on a nearby institution, but few banks had been as progressive or as sound as this long-established stronghold on the Jersey seacoast. One of the first to make consumer loans, elect a woman officer, and provide generous employee benefits, the institution was thought to be as sound as the United States Treasury.

"Who's doing it? Who's responsible?" Paul wanted to know, unable to believe that the bank was unsafe. Taking out his money was like having to rescue all of one's possessions from a house threatened by a five-alarm fire. The young teller thought of his wife and their two small children and his stomach sickened. Tonight he and Mary were going to do the Christmas shopping, but—

"Get it while you can," Burt urged. "I took all mine, but don't tell anyone I told you!"

Hastily Paul filled out a withdrawal slip and returned to his stool. He counted out the money in tens until he had a stack of twelve bills. Then he added four ones and a half dollar, making a total of $124.50. That was all the money Mary and he had. He experienced a queer feeling as he rolled the cash into a wad and shoved it into his back trouser pocket. It was the first time that he could remember when he did not have any money in a bank.

The minute Burt relieved him for lunch, Paul hurried to the nearest telephone booth to call his wife.

"Mary, there's a run on the bank! It's terrible! Don't tell a soul, but call your father right away and tell him to get down here and withdraw his money. I got ours. You should see the lines of people. It can't last much longer!"

When he returned to his cage, the lines reached out farther than before.

"We called the Federal Reserve for help," Burt whispered, "but I don't think they can do much."

"Then what will happen?" Paul's eyes searched Burt's face for an answer. This had been Paul's only job. After high school he had started as a messenger in the bank, worked his way up to a clerical position, and then to teller. Everyone had said you couldn't find a safer job than in a bank.

"We'll never have to worry," he had told Mary when he proposed to her. While others had lost their jobs after the market crash, Paul had not been concerned. The country had to have banks, and his was one of the best.

"Here's your money." He pushed a pile of twenties toward another depositor who grabbed it as though he thought Paul might change his mind and take the bills back. Paul glanced down at his cash drawer and frowned. He would soon need more currency.

Suddenly a tall bald man pushed his way to the head of the line.

"Close your window. Close it right away." The voice was one of authority, but the face was unfamiliar. Paul blinked rapidly but did not move.

"Close up," the man said. "Orders from the state banking department."

Paul slowly swung the little glass door shut, and in so doing dashed the hopes of all those in the lobby who also sought to withdraw their money.

"Close up, close up," the auditor repeated to the other tellers.

One by one the windows shut. It was so quiet that the click of each snapping lock could be heard throughout the bank. Then, when the depositors realized what this meant, a faint buzzing gradually grew to a roar. Some distraught men and women shouted to have the windows opened, others wept, and many, heads lowered, silently made their way outdoors.

"What will we do?" Mary asked, as Paul opened the front door that evening.

"We're lucky, dear," he reassured her. "They said there's plenty of work straightening out the accounts. They think the bank will open soon. How about your father? Did he make it in time?"

Mary shook her head slowly. "He's wiped out. Everything he had was there. You know how he trusted that bank, especially with you working in it. I guess there's only one answer?" she blinked back the tears as she looked up.

Paul nodded. It meant another mouth to feed, but at least he had his job and they could take care of the old man.

A few weeks later an officer called Paul to his desk. "I don't know how to tell you this, Paul." He looked away as he spoke. "I'm sorry, but we're all done. The bank isn't reopening now. It's the end for all of us."

"You—you don't—"

"Afraid I do. I don't know what to suggest. Sorry. We'll mail your check."

Shoulders bent, his eyes open but not seeing, Paul Anderson slowly walked back to his desk. Mechanically he picked up his glasses, put on his overcoat, and went out into the snow. It was like the end of the world.

Bank failures were not unusual. Even before the depression, during the period 1921–1929 which included the boom days, almost six thousand banks had closed temporarily or forever. From 1930 through 1932, another six thousand had failed, most of them in very small cities and towns. More than half of them had operated with capital of less than twenty-five thousand dollars. Deflation had set in since the market crash, and people were slowly converting property into bank deposits so that the banks were literally bursting with money. Corporations, too, were reporting increased amounts of "cash on hand or in bank," and savings bank deposits reached new heights because, unlike land, jewelry, and numerous commodities, money was the only thing that had not depreciated in value.

It was not for lack of money that many banks closed. Often it was management ineptitude or dishonesty, loans that could not be liquidated, or, most unfortunate of all, rumors. Such was the case in Morgantown, West Virginia, after mergers and suspensions had closed seven of the city's banks.

THE MORGANTOWN PLAN

Closed for Liquidation, the sign on the door of the Bank of Morgantown read. It was the eighth institution to close, and now the county was without a single bank. Although the bank had a substantial amount of cash and assets which exceeded its deposits, the officers could not liquidate loans fast enough to meet the demands of terrified depositors who had listened to false rumors and wanted their money. The directors reasoned that it was better to close the bank and save what they had.

A novel plan devised by William John, a Morgantown

attorney, for saving the bank was announced in the newspapers. Local bankers said that it would rescue the bank, provided that the stockholders and the depositors agreed to it. Under the terms of his proposal, depositors would leave their funds intact for a year in order to give the community an opportunity to regain its economic equilibrium. During this time, stockholders would waive dividends but depositors were to be paid interest on their "protected" deposits. After the twelve-month period they might withdraw a fifth of their funds every three months.

The owners and depositors agreed to the plan, whereupon the bank reopened. Immediately the newspapers were deluged with calls from other banks in distress whose managements were anxious to try anything in order to keep from failing and who wanted full details of the plan that was so successful in Morgantown.

Paradoxically, the Reconstruction Finance Corporation received the most blame for the bank closings, this being the agency which had been established principally to save banks by lending money on collateral that was sound but difficult to market. Congress had insisted that it be told of every loan and for the Washington newspaper reporter this was news. When home-town depositors read that their bank had borrowed from the R.F.C., they became alarmed.

Others said that Congress' failure to balance the budget was responsible for bank failures. They claimed that shrewd international bankers made heavy withdrawals of gold from the United States because they anticipated that the country was about to enter an inflationary period.

In 1931, the public's previous enthusiasm for putting cash into the banks gradually began to diminish as people started to hoard. Bank deposits shrank twelve billion dollars between 1930 and 1933 and the practice of hoarding gained momentum until February, 1933, when a new wave hit the country. At that time, when there was widespread poverty, unemployment, and want, specie in circulation rose by more than nine hundred million dollars. It was the largest amount of money in the hands of Americans the country had ever known. Convinced that they would lose all their savings if left in banks, enough people preferred the privacy of their mattresses to bank vaults to trigger a banking crisis. Little wonder that on Wednesday morning, February 14, 1933, the radio carried bad news.

The Bank Closings

"Every bank in Michigan has been ordered closed by Governor Comstock for eight days," the radio announcer said. "The action is purely precautionary. There is no cause for alarm."

Actually, there was good reason to worry because the important Detroit National Bank was in serious trouble. Had the Governor not proclaimed the holiday there was real danger that runs might start. Few people realized that Michigan was not the first state to close its banks. Nevada had experienced a twelve-day bank moratorium the previous November.

No sooner had depositors in other states learned of the Michigan closings than many, fearing that the same thing might happen to them, rushed to get their money. Ugly rumors, most without foundation, frightened people who should have known better than to join their neighbors in a mad rush to withdraw all their deposits. In city after city runs began as fear generated fear, and depositors, their deadpan faces masking inner terror, formed long lines before banks. One sound institution after another failed because it lacked enough money to meet all the withdrawal demands. A bank holiday was ordered by the Governor of Maryland. Then the chief executives of Ohio, Indiana, Kentucky, and Pennsylvania issued the same order.

"The unthinking attempt of the public to convert over forty billions of dollars of deposits into currency at one time is, on its face, impossible," declared an official of the New York Clearing House Association.

The bank holiday in Michigan was extended beyond the first eight days, and in Detroit alone some seven hundred million dollars was frozen. The large automobile manufacturers were forced to import cash from wherever they could obtain it to meet payrolls, and New York City banks shipped funds to commercial customers in Detroit. Plans were made to issue scrip money to relieve the situation, but were abandoned for fear of counterfeiting.

Michigan seemed to be having more than its share of troubles until the rest of the country suddenly found itself in the same situation. One day in San Francisco a well-dressed man pushed a check toward the teller.

The other man glanced nervously about him, then whispered cautiously: "I'd take everything I had, Mr. Whitely. I heard they're going to close every bank in the country."

His eyes wide with fright, the depositor quickly wrote another check, grabbed the wad of bills and fled.

It was Friday, March 3, 1933, the last day of Herbert Hoover's term in office—a day that might well have been called Black Friday. There was hardly a state in which some banks were not closed or partially shut. In Indiana, withdrawals were limited to 5 per cent of a depositor's bank balance as of February 25th. A new law in Pennsylvania required depositors to document the reasons for their withdrawals. A third of the circulating money had disappeared after anxious Americans took gold and bank notes and hid them. Little wonder that men and women, frightened by rumors of insolvency and news of dangerous drains on bank deposits, lost their confidence in our nation's banks as one sound institution after another was forced to suspend operations.

In Chicago and New York, people jammed the banks from nine until three, demanding their money. Leading bankers sent telegrams to President Hoover warning that they could not continue to pay out deposits without adequate cash reserves. It looked as though the country's financial structure had collapsed.

The following morning, Herbert Hoover sat at his desk in the White House winding up his official duties. His face was haggard and he was exhausted after working steadily for forty-eight hours. Word had just come in that Governor Herbert Lehman had closed all the banks in New York State and that the Governor of Illinois had done the same.

"We are at the end of our string—there is nothing more we can do," he remarked wearily to his aide.

At five minutes after eleven, in accord with tradition, a black limousine drew up to the White House. In it were Mr. and Mrs. Franklin Delano Roosevelt, who had come to make a last call on the outgoing President. Mr. Hoover spared the crippled Roosevelt the inconvenience of leaving his car. Instead he shook hands and talked with his visitors for a few minutes, then entered the car and rode with the President-elect and his wife down Pennsylvania Avenue, past half a million cheering men, women, and children to the stand that had been erected before the Capitol. Here some hundred and fifty thousand people were on hand to watch the inauguration ceremonies.

"There is nothing to fear but fear itself," President Roosevelt told the throng gathered before him and the unseen millions huddled anxiously about their radios.

The Bank Holiday

Early the next morning, only a short time after the last guests had left the inaugural ball, the President held his first cabinet meeting. Later he issued the following proclamation:

> WHEREAS: There have been heavy and unwarranted withdrawals of gold and currency from our banking institutions for purposes of hoarding and
>
> WHEREAS: Continuous and extensive speculative activity abroad has resulted in a severe drain on this nation's stocks of gold,
>
> THEREFORE, I, Franklin D. Roosevelt, President of the United States of America, in order to prevent export, hoarding or earmarking of gold and silver bullion or currency, do hereby proclaim that from Monday, March 6, 1933, to Monday, March 13, 1933, there shall be maintained a bank holiday.

Thus, on Monday, March 6th, for the first time in America's history, not a single bank opened. Trading on the New York Stock Exchange and the Chicago Board of Trade was suspended. The nation's economic wheels had stopped. It was an uncanny, chilling feeling to realize that you could not get money—your money—when you wanted it. On the other hand, the bank closings were like the comic relief that comes late in a gripping drama. For the first time since the depression had begun, everyone shared a common problem. Rich and poor alike were denied access to banks, and even those on relief whose bank balances had long since disappeared felt a certain tie with those who had funds on deposit but could not use them. Despite the crisis, life suddenly became an adventure for many, as they tapped their ingenuity to see how they could live without money.

A traveling salesman who had to go to Chicago hurried up to the ticket window at Washington's Union Depot. Pointing to his checkbook, he explained that he lacked money for a ticket.

"You'll have to pay cash," the clerk told him. "We aren't allowed to accept checks."

This man was not as unfortunate as Americans stranded in Montreal, who found that their dollars and travelers' checks were valueless while banks in the United States were closed. Some tourists were in near panic. They could neither buy tickets to get home nor use their money to purchase food or lodging while they remained in Canada.

Every savings bank throughout the United States had closed, thus cutting off cash that would have helped many a frugal person through this difficult period. The thrifty who had put their money in savings banks in anticipation of a rainy day were even worse off than those who used checking accounts. A number of banks invoked a seldom-used rule that required depositors to give them sixty days advance notice before they could withdraw money from their accounts.

Ministers, fortunately, understood the problem. In one church, the collection was suspended altogether. In another, the trustees passed the word around that they would gladly accept checks, and from the pulpit of a third, the pastor urged his parishioners to put I.O.U.'s in the plate.

Meanwhile, many farmers threatened to stop milk shipments unless paid in cash. Concerned lest they be unable to buy food, people jammed the markets, causing a sudden rise in grocery sales. The Grand Union grocery chain announced plans to issue coupon books redeemable at their stores, the books to be sold to business firms and given employees in part payment of wages.

Large old bills and rare coins appeared as men and women reached under rugs, into cookie jars and other hiding places for cash. Even those lucky few who had plenty of paper money were unable to use it to telephone, ride a bus, buy a newspaper, or make other purchases, because they could not get it changed. In fact, change became so scarce that people resorted to all kinds of tricks to break large banknotes. Long lines formed in railroad stations as men and women offered hundred-, five-hundred-, and even thousand-dollar bills for twenty-five-cent tickets they had no intention of using. When shopkeepers in an Illinois town heard that a thrifty boy had saved $113.57 in pennies, they rushed to his house and refused to leave until they had exchanged their bills for his precious copper coins. Millionaire John D. Rockefeller, who gave away dimes, rapidly ran out of coins and had to give his caddy a dollar bill instead of the usual dime.

By Wednesday, March 8th, cash had become even more scarce, but Secretary Woodin ruled against issuing scrip.

"We don't need it," he said, fearful of substituting anything that resembled stage money. "We can issue currency against sound assets of banks."

Officials in numerous cities and states did not agree, and they began to issue paper scrip to be used in place of cash until the banks reopened. In New Jersey, George H. La Monte & Sons' paper mill went from a three-day work week to a twenty-hour day, trying to keep up with orders for paper to be used in printing scrip. Postage stamps, streetcar tickets, Mexican silver, and even slugs were used for money. In many areas, farm produce was accepted in place of cash and one legislator arrived at his state capital carrying a side of pork and a dozen eggs to keep him through the week.

"Live and dine on your checkbook," advertised Manhattan's Hotels Commodore and Biltmore. Franklin Simon in New York invited new charge accounts and advertised that checks were acceptable in payment of bills.

One place a check was worthless was at the post office.

"Sorry, not allowed to take checks unless they're certified," the postmaster told a leading businessman who needed stamps.

"But how can I get this check certified when the bank's closed?" the man asked.

In Kansas, the state ordered insurance underwriters to allow thirty extra grace days for payment of life insurance premiums.

The bank holiday dragged on through Thursday, Friday, and Saturday while exhausted government officials remained at their desks trying to decide which banks were sound enough to reopen.

People throughout America now felt the pinch of having no cash.

Detroit was in an especially ugly mood. People in the Motor City were not spending. Stores were deserted, restaurants were practically empty.

"Do you know what they're doing?" one restaurant owner asked, and then answered his own question. "They're buying ham and cheese and taking them home." The only business he had was from customers he knew and who signed their food checks with a written promise to pay later when they had cash.

Fifty people were scattered inside a movie theater that normally had an attendance of over a thousand in that pretelevision era.

Of the Motor City's nineteen hundred municipal laborers, half could not find any way to cash their checks. Every day more and more people were fainting on the job from malnutrition.

And for the two thousand patients in a tuberculosis sanitarium, the day came when there was enough food on hand for only six more meals.

On Sunday, March 13th, the whole nation held its breath. That evening at ten o'clock, Washington time, President Roosevelt gave the first of his famous radio "fireside chats."

He reviewed the "bad banking situation," explained the steps that the government had taken to restore confidence, and promised that the twelve Federal Reserve banks would issue currency as fast as they could. This would be good currency, backed by sound assets of stable banks. It was planned that in each of the twelve Federal Reserve cities certain banks would open the next day. Institutions in 250 other cities would admit customers on Tuesday, and on Wednesday another group of eligible banks could resume business.

"I do not promise you that every bank will be reopened or that individual losses will not be suffered," he declared, "but there will be no losses that possibly could be avoided; and there would have been more and greater losses had we continued to operate."

One man who listened anxiously to the speech was A. P. Giannini, head of the giant Bank of America in California. He had just returned from Washington, where he had been consulting with top government banking officials. Calling his bank "the cleanest bank in the country," he confidently expected that it would be allowed to reopen on Monday morning. In fact, he knew that, because of the bank's size and importance to the whole western part of the country, it *must* reopen. For its doors to remain closed when other banks were permitted to reopen would undoubtedly invite disaster for that part of the nation.

But the hours sped by and no word came. Throughout the night long-distance telephone wires hummed between San Francisco and Washington as call after call pleaded the bank's case and argued that it was in sound condition and must be permitted to open Monday morning. For a time it looked as though the problem would be referred to the White House and that President Roosevelt would have to be awakened to decide the matter. Finally, at 6:30 A.M., Washington time, the Secretary of the Treasury agreed to license the bank's reopening. With but six hours' time left, Giannini and his staff went to work to make certain that business would be resumed at the regular time that morning.

And what happened after the bank's huge doors swung open? Mr. Giannini and the other officers watched tensely as the banking floor gradually filled with a crowd of men and women. Later, Giannini toured the branches and at the end of the day reported to Washington that "normal banking conditions prevailed everywhere. On my visits to our branches I found depositors cheerful and most willing to cooperate in the President's policies."

Across the nation in Philadelphia, the president of the Philadelphia National Bank, which was among the first banks permitted to reopen, stated:

"Everything seems to be running very smoothly today and the announcement from Washington, particularly the radio address of the President last evening, appears to have produced good results, and today money is fast pouring back into the bank."

A holiday spirit swept the Quaker City. A sigh of relief wafted across the land. Three days later, when 162 banks in Michigan reopened and bankers there found that deposits exceeded withdrawals, everyone knew that the banking crisis was over.

All the banks were not considered strong enough to reopen, however. The experience of a commercial bank in a northern industrial city was typical of what happened to numerous shaky institutions.

SIGN UP OR ELSE

"Mrs. Graham? I'm Henry Purcell of the First National Bank. May I come in for a moment?"

The elderly widow admitted the bank officer and motioned him to a chair.

"When is the bank going to reopen?" she wanted to know. "The bank holiday's been over for a month and our bank is still closed."

"That is why I'm here," Mr. Purcell said. "We have to call on every one of our depositors, and it takes a long time."

He then explained that, because the bank had so much money tied up in loans and mortgages, the Federal government had ruled that before it could reopen, the officers would have to withhold 20 per cent of all the deposits. In return for the money put into the bank's reserves, each depositor would receive bank stock of equivalent value. Thus, a person with a thousand dollars on deposit would have eight hundred dollars cash and two hundred dollars' worth of stock. "We expect to buy back the stock soon and of course we will pay dividends on it," Mr. Purcell promised. "We cannot reopen unless most of the depositors agree to this arrangement. Actually, we're better off than some banks. The Commercial Trust is releasing only 50 per cent of its depositors' money and forcing them to take the other half in bank stock."

"Suppose I don't sign this agreement?" Mrs. Graham asked.

"Twenty per cent of your money will be withheld anyway and you won't get any bank stock."

"Then I guess I have no choice." She shook her head sadly, thinking of the two thousand dollars that would no longer be in her account. "All right. Give me the agreement."

Most of the depositors agreed to sign, the stock was issued, and the bank reopened. Although dividends were paid regularly, the shares were never repurchased by the bank and they had no value. Five years after the bank holiday the doors closed again, this time forever, but there was a difference.

In June, 1933, Congress had created the Federal Deposit Insurance Corporation (FDIC), which insured small depositors to the extent of twenty-five hundred dollars. (This sum was increased to five thousand dollars in 1934 and is now fifteen thousand dollars.) Now officials of the FDIC took charge of the bank. Although the bank stock which depositors held was worthless, money which had been on deposit was quickly made available to customers in amounts up to five thousand dollars, the maximum amount covered by the FDIC insurance. Everyone was reconciled to the situation except one little old lady who had an account with five dollars on deposit.

When she was given a crisp five-dollar bill, she bridled. "What do you mean, giving me *that?*" she asked. "I know all about insurance! My husband was an agent." She pointed to the small sign by the teller's window. "It says that accounts are insured up to five thousand dollars. All right, the bank closed. So now give me my five thousand dollars!"

8

THE ILL-HOUSED

Eviction

High up on the fire escape of a theater in a large city,
cleverly concealed behind the bars and protected by an
overhanging tin roof, a man had built himself a home,
using cardboard for the walls and floor and a thin pallet
for a bed. Too old to work but too proud to be a public
charge, the man climbed down from his home early in
the morning, washed in a public rest room and spent the
day vainly hunting work. The bread line provided food,
and each night he returned to his "home" to sleep there.

As might be expected, the building inspector finally
discovered the little room with its neatly printed sign:

PLEASE DO NOT DISTURB. I AM HOMELESS
AND SEEKING A JOB. I BOTHER NO ONE.

That night at the police station the captain read his orders to the night force.

"Murphy, the building inspector filed a violation against the Bijou Theater. Some bum's living up on the fire escape. Throw him out."

An hour later, the policeman approached the theater and looked up at the stairway. In the dark it was impossible to see the cardboard house. He thought of the man and of his own home and family and walked on.

"Nobody was there," he lied to his superior when he returned to the stationhouse.

"Then get him tomorrow," the captain barked.

The next night while the policeman stood in the shadows watching the theater, putting off the deed, he saw an old man cross the street. He walked erect, he was neatly dressed, and he was very thin. As he neared the theater he looked up and down the street, then hurried toward the fire escape.

"Hey, you! Where are you going?" Murphy called.

"Nowhere," the man said.

"Up the stairs to that shack?" the cop asked.

The man nodded slowly. He looked so helpless and alone.

The policeman walked toward him. "I hate to do this to you," he said, "but you're trespassing and it's against the law to block a fire escape."

"I know," the old man admitted, "but I wasn't doing any harm. I haven't any place to go. Can't I stay just for tonight? I'll go first thing in the morning."

The policeman hesitated. What would he tell the captain? Another night wouldn't hurt, but if the sergeant came around, well—he just couldn't afford to lose his job.

"Afraid not, you've got to go sooner or later. Orders are orders," he said briskly. "I'll help you get the stuff down if you want."

"No, there's not that much. I can manage."

Five minutes later Officer Murphy watched the old man shuffle off into the dark, a little pallet over one shoulder, a pack of cardboard in the other hand. Like thousands of others he would continue to wander from place to place.

Murphy shook his head as he rubbed his nightstick thoughtfully. What harm was the old man doing up there, he wondered. Why all that fuss? The theater had been closed for over a year.

Late in September, 1930, a thousand men were resting on the lower level of Michigan Avenue sprawled along a loading platform of one of the skyscrapers. Twelve months later the Commissioner of Public Welfare reported that hundreds of homeless women were sleeping nightly in the parks.

The depression was not a year old before fifteen hundred men were dozing in doorways and out-of-the-way hideouts in Pittsburgh.

Still affluent commuters making their way to New York's Grand Central Station passed through corridors that were lined with homeless men stretched out on the floor.

In every city across the nation from Boston to San Francisco, from St. Paul to Houston, there were homeless, unemployed men and women. A woman had difficulty traveling from city to city without money. On the other hand, a man could hop a freight, live in hobo "jungles," and somehow find an occasional meal. He might sleep in a packing case, an empty barrel, an unused sewer pipe, a deserted building, or even within a coffin as a Bonus

Marcher did. In the morning, he would visit the city dump and vie with others for scraps of salvageable garbage or pieces of clothing that still could be worn.

The Hoovervilles

The more fortunate dispossessed men lived in "Hoovervilles." Every city had one or more of these squalid collections of haphazardly erected shacks made of discarded packing cases, tin, tarpaper, cardboard, and wood. During the summer these communities were hot, dirty, smelly, sometimes muddy and always a health threat, since there were neither sanitary facilities nor running water. In winter the shacks were cold, usually unheated, and unfit for habitation in climates far from tropical.

HOOVER VALLEY

"Mike! Look what I got today!" Butch Kruger, a tall gaunt man, smiled as he held up a piece of serviceable brown carpeting. "Found it over near Park Avenue on top of an ash can. Now I'll live in style!"

"Not for long." Mike shook his head. "They're going to kick us out."

"Who said so? They can't do it. Where would we go?"

"Board of Health told the cops we ain't sanitary 'cause we have to use the public comfort stations."

"Well, I'm not giving up this place, not I! First decent home I've had in two years. Just let them try!"

He looked with pride at his little house made of bricks which he had carted, six at a time, from a lot near the park. With an old iron bedstead, a table, a chair, and an oil lamp, his was one of the most pretentious of the seventeen shacks that stood on "Depression Street."

One of the finest Hoovervilles, this community nicknamed Hoover Valley by the Park Department, had sprung up during the summer of 1932 at the south end of New York City's Central Park reservoir. Unmolested by the police, the residents decided to winterize their shacks with more permanent building materials since this was a pleasant place to live.

The finest building in Hoover Valley was a brick affair, twenty feet high, nestled against a huge boulder. Unemployed bricklayers had built it, topped it with a roof of inlaid tile and named it Rockside Inn. A nearby shack constructed of egg and fruit crates flew a tattered American flag from its flat roof. A sign by the flimsy door read *Radio City*. It contained the Valley's only radio and was always open to all citizens of that community.

"It was just a rumor you heard," Butch said that evening, as he and Mike listened to the news in Radio City. "They wouldn't have let us go to all this work if they weren't going to let us stay."

A moment later there was a hesitant rap on the door.

"Open up! Order of the Park Commissioner." Then a well-tanned policeman stepped inside. He was obviously embarrassed.

"Bad news, boys," he said. "Orders of the Park Commissioner. We've got to lock you all up for vagrancy." He paused and looked down at his worn black shoes. "Tomorrow they're going to knock 'em all down. No running water, no toilets. That's the reason, he says."

A hand reached over and turned off the radio, but otherwise no one moved. Too stunned to speak, the men merely stared into space, unable to believe or accept what the officer had said.

"You can go get your things before we leave for the stationhouse," the cop added. Then he stepped outside.

The homeless were not the only ones to suffer dispossession. It happened to countless people who lived in good houses, too.

FOUR WEEKS TO GO

The Daniel Richmonds lived in a comfortable home in a western city. Every Saturday night the family could tell whether or not Mr. Richmond had sold many life insurance policies that week. If he had made his quota there were flowers under one arm for his wife and a phonograph record, a book, or a box of candy under the other for the three children. If he had not reached the goal set by the office, he brought home only his bulging briefcase.

After the crash of October, 1929, Mr. Richmond brought the flowers and other gifts for a few weeks, but by Christmas he carried only the briefcase. It became increasingly difficult to locate prospects who could afford to buy insurance. Just as bad, clients who had purchased policies could not pay the premiums. As policyholders let their insurance lapse, Mr. Richmond lost most of his income. Soon he was deep in debt, as he borrowed constantly just to buy food and coal. Since he had made no payments on the mortgage for over a year, one day he received the expected letter requesting him to come to the bank.

"Mr. Richmond"—the officer leaned back in his leather chair and rested his chin on his fingertips—"we're going to have to foreclose unless you can pay at least a thousand dollars toward what you owe."

"A thousand dollars! That's impossible! You—you mean you're going to put us out of our house?" Mr. Richmond had always considered it *their* house. Now it was the bank's property.

"That's what I mean. We can't carry the property any longer without payments. We'll give you three to four weeks to pay up or get out."

It was no use. Mr. Richmond could not think where to take the family. He and his wife talked late into the night, but they arrived at no solution. At the end of the four weeks there was nothing they could do but move into his sister's house. There the children slept in the dining room and the parents used the couch in the living room.

This was the usual pattern—families losing their homes and moving in with relatives. In some cases, three or four people slept in a bed and after the family had sold off its furniture to buy food there was no place to sit.

A Philadelphia social worker testified before a Senate committee that "only the other day a family of ten moved in with a family of five in a three-room apartment. The demand for boxes on which people can sit or stretch themselves is hardly to be believed."

The Richmonds were more fortunate than the average family which could not pay its rent and was evicted more promptly. Public sympathy usually lay with the tenants, not the landlords, and often an eviction would start a neighborhood riot. Usually, the family would carry its few pitiful pieces of furniture and lumpy mattresses down the stairs, throw them on a cart or a truck, and go to another slum tenement. Here they would pay a few dollars' rent in advance and stay until the sheriff dispossessed them once again. For some families this was such a normal occurrence that the children played a game of "eviction" with their dolls and doll furniture.

Although sheriffs evicted 273,000 families from their

Men became migrants and lived in shanties, rode the freight cars, and ate in soup kitchens. When they could they applied for relief checks. Others, with nothing to do, dispiritedly played checkers or cards in some of the rooms set up by charitable organizations. *The Print and Picture Department, The Free Library of Philadelphia*

These men were part of the army of 350,000 being added to the WPA rolls in 1937 as the Federal Government moved to take up with "made work" the slack of private employment accompanying the business recession that year. The men in this photograph were part of the 5,000 who would soon switch over to WPA payrolls in Cleveland, Ohio. *Acme*

In April, 1940, some 2,000 unemployed gathered on the steps of the Los Angeles City Hall and demanded that the government lower appropriations for armaments and give them higher relief checks. The observance was for "National Re-employment Day," and the members stood quietly and listened to speeches by local leaders, as well as a radio speech by David Lasser, Workers Alliance president. *Acme*

The plight of families in the South was as desperate as that of those in the urban centers of the North and the West. Poverty was acute among the farmers, many of whom had nothing to plant and no place to sell the crops if they did plant them.
The Print and Picture Department, The Free Library of Philadelphia

homes in 1932, all landlords were not heartless. Many let tenants remain in apartments and homes even though they could not pay the rent. Some apartment and home owners suffered more than their penniless tenants because, although they might have no income from rents to pay their bills and buy food, they could not qualify for relief as long as they owned property.

Good and bad housing alike stood empty. Throughout the nation it was difficult to find lessors for luxury apartments or homes. Many of the old mansions were deserted, and, because they were not suitable for conversion into nonresidential uses, the banks that held their mortgages found them practically valueless. With so much property unrented or standing empty, tax collections fell off and cities lost much of their principal source of income.

Residential construction dropped so drastically that in 1932 it amounted to only 15 per cent of what it had been before the crash. People could not afford new homes at a time when families were doubling up. In the poorest sections, although underprivileged families living in horrible tenements needed better housing, there were no funds to provide it.

People living on farms did not enjoy luxury living, either. In the year that marked the start of the depression, the average value of the 776,000 dwellings occupied by sharecroppers was only $283. Only 15 per cent of all farms had piped in water and 13 per cent enjoyed the convenience of electricity. Since farmers had suffered from overproduction and low prices for many years, it was natural that they should be unable to maintain their homes properly or improve their property.

The New Deal for Housing

When the new Democratic administration took office in March, 1933, there were many emergency problems to be solved. One of the most urgent concerned home owners. Every day a thousand families were losing their residences.

HELPING THE HOMEOWNER

In 1932, Congress had established the Federal Home Loan Bank System with twelve regional branches like the Federal Reserve System. Its purpose was to stop further mortgage foreclosures by making loans available to home owners, but since it loaned only 50 per cent of the value of the property, few took advantage of it.

Relief to the home owners in peril of foreclosure came in 1933 from the newly created Home Owners Loan Corporation which refinanced mortgages and made it possible for owners to keep their property. Further help came in 1934 through the Federal Housing Administration (FHA), which made available insured mortgages with low interest rates and long periods for repayment. It also provided loans for home owners who wanted to repair or improve their property. This financing is still handled by local banking institutions which make the actual loans after they have secured the government's assurance that it will make good on any unpaid installments. The borrower pays a small fee, one-half of 1 per cent, as a premium to support a mortgage insurance fund which has always been sufficient to pay off loans which were in default.

ELIMINATING THE SLUMS

By 1930, slums had blighted large areas of many cities. It was evident that slum clearance was long overdue and that substandard obsolete housing should be replaced with modern housing designed for low-income families.

A token beginning was made by the Reconstruction Finance Corporation when it offered to lend money in 1932 for various public works projects. New York was the only city that requested money for a new housing development. With the establishment of the Public Works Administration in 1933, numerous projects provided for the erection of modern housing on slum sites. Unfortunately, many of these new apartments were priced too high for the families that lived in the former slums. Nevertheless, as fifty-one projects were constructed in thirty-six cities, progress was achieved in eliminating some of the most notorious slum areas, such as the "Bloody 18th Ward" in Chicago, the "Greasy Plank" district of Memphis, Atlanta's "Beaver Slide," "Whiskey Island" in Cleveland, and various disreputable areas in New York City.

One blighted section that PWA money rebuilt was near the New Orleans docks. Here stood Bedbug Row, Buzzards, The Yellow Dog, The Red Devil, and other rows of substandard, rotting, rat-infested houses. Monthly rentals were four dollars a room and up. Running water and toilets were available—in the back yards. In some places, as many as forty people shared two broken-down, filthy privies.

In 1937, President Roosevelt called an extraordinary session of Congress. He informed the legislators that housing construction had failed to keep pace with the nation's needs or the population expansion. He saw the need for at least six to eight hundred thousand new dwelling units costing twelve to sixteen billion dollars annually during the next five years. While assisting the construction industry, not only would new homes be provided but also all business would be stimulated, national income would rise, and unemployment would be reduced.

The Wagner-Steagall National Housing Act of 1937 was the administration's program for solving the housing problem in a comprehensive manner and not as part of an over-all public works or recovery program. Instead of actually erecting apartment houses and other buildings as the PWA did, the new United States Housing Authority was prepared to lend to local housing agencies up to 100 per cent of the cost of housing projects. During the next four years, it spent seven hundred and fifty million dollars to finance 511 projects that provided over 161,000 living units. After 1941, the agency concentrated on providing housing for defense workers, but a good beginning had been made in rebuilding our cities.

9

THE BOY AND GIRL WANDERERS

Larry Giles huddled miserably in the corner of the dark, swaying boxcar. Tall for a fifteen-year-old, he had a slight frame, light hair, and a smiling face. It was necessary to brace himself to keep from sliding on the cold steel floor as the car swayed around first one curve and then another. He wished that the doors were closed because it was getting cold and he had nothing warm to wear besides his blue sweater. From time to time, as the car passed a station or a street light, he could see the older boy who lay on the floor near him. The youth appeared to be about his own height and build. In contrast to Larry's neat clothes, the other boy's jacket and pants were ragged and torn. In the flickering light he could see that the boy's toes stuck out from his canvas sneakers.

"You from St. Louis?" the boy called above the roar and *clackety, clack* of the wheels.

"How did you know?" It was the first time Larry had left the city, but he did not want to admit it.

"By the way you climbed into the car when we stopped there for water and coal. Why'd you come? Where are you going?"

Larry was homesick already and preferred not to talk, but it was good to have some companionship.

"Dad's been out of work since last year," he said. "Somebody had to leave and I'm the oldest, so he gave me ten dollars and told me to go to California for the winter. There wasn't enough food for all of us children."

"You got ten dollars on you?"

Immediately Larry realized his mistake. He must be more careful.

Then the voice called: "It's O.K., kid. I won't take it off you, but don't tell anyone else. They might want it for themselves."

"Thanks. Where are you from?" It was only hospitable to return the question.

"Pittsburgh was my home. Been on the road two years, ever since I graduated from high school. There were no jobs, so I hitchhiked out West and I've been going ever since. You can't hitchhike any more, though, so I ride the rails. Haven't found a job either." He buttoned the thin jacket about him. "Name's Tom Spanik. Going to take a nap now before the next stop. Never know how long you can stay aboard."

He pulled a cap down over his face and rolled on his side, leaving Larry alone with his thoughts of home and the dread of the unknown ahead. He had no plan, no idea of where he should go, or, for that matter, where the train was heading. It had seemed like a great adventure when his father suggested the trip, but now he was not so sure. Nevertheless, in spite of the cold, the hard bumping floor under him, and his anxiety, he dozed.

Suddenly he was awake. A bright light shone in his face and he was aware that the train had stopped.

"Hey, you guys in there! Get out!" The voice was gruff and insistent.

Tom stirred, turned on his back and sat up.

"Hurry up, get going!"

The boys struggled to their feet. Larry followed Tom unsteadily to the door. He was too frightened to think for himself and jumped to the ground at Tom's side.

"How many times we got to tell you not to ride these trains? Now get off the tracks and scram! And don't come back!"

Glaring floodlights lighted the large railroad yard. The tracks were dotted with freight cars, and not far away a steam engine was chugging toward them. Clutching his brown paper bag, Larry stumbled over the rails close behind Tom. He saw other men and boys leaving the train.

"Follow me, kid," Tom called over his shoulder, as they reached the edge of the yard. He made his way through heavy underbrush and out into an open clearing. It was early dawn, and Larry could barely see the outline of a field.

"We'll stay here and wait till the cops go away. Then we'll go back and hop another freight."

"Can't we get something to eat?" Larry asked. "I'm hungry."

"When did you eat last?"

"Supper."

"Then you're not hungry. You're not hungry till you haven't eaten for two days."

"Can't we find a restaurant just the same? I'll buy you breakfast, too."

Tom sat on a stump and shook his finger at the younger boy. "You aren't hungry, I told you. You aren't hungry till your stomach's so empty it reaches up and grabs your throat and till your legs are so flabby they won't work. That's when you buy a meal—if you have any money. Thanks, anyway, but I'm not hungry. Had some soup and bread at a mission before I climbed on that train."

Larry and Tom were part of the army of young people estimated to number as many as three hundred thousand. They were on the march, and although called "homeless," some social workers doubted that more than 5 per cent were really without a home. About 90 per cent were boys, the balance girls, teen-age and some older. Many of the young people on the road were like Larry, who left home because there was not enough food. Others, like Tom, were seeking jobs, and there were also those who sought adventure and something to do to kill time. The boys ranged in age upward from the twelve-year-old who lived in the New York City subway system for months, existing on scraps and skins found in refuse cans. Approximately 25 per cent of the youths were under twenty-one. A number came from good homes, and some were college graduates.

When boys began to leave their families in 1930 and wander across the nation, they did not use the freights like the traditional hoboes. They were not bums, but for the most part impoverished young people seeking jobs, and it was natural that they should ask for rides from motorists. They were usually successful in obtaining transportation, but so many were killed or hurt by careless hit-and-run drivers that eventually most of them took to the rails. Here some were maimed and others lost their lives, but the accident rate was lower.

The first girls to take to the road were those who hitch-hiked from resort to resort looking for seasonal work. When no jobs materialized, they too switched from highways to railways, seeking protection and safety by joining with gangs of boy tramps of their own age. They lived like tribes. The boys begged, bought, or stole the food which the girls cooked. The boys also obtained such clothing and other necessities as the girls required. Most of the boys and young men on the road had nothing to do with these mixed groups, however, Larry and Tom being among them.

The two boys returned to the yard later that morning and cautiously looked out from the bushes.

"See that train there?" Tom pointed up the track. "Engine's hooking on to it now. Means they'll be leaving soon."

He told Larry exactly how to board a freight that is just starting, why you must face forward whenever boarding or leaving a moving car, and where to look for handholds. Boxcars with open doors offer the best ride; next safest is a gondola, though it affords no protection from bad weather, and flat cars without sides are least preferable.

"One thing," Tom warned, "if you jump on a train between the cars by the couplings, don't hit the cutting lever! It separates the train and sets the brakes. Once I saw a girl climb on a train. She hit the lever and when the train jolted she fell off and—understand?"

Because most of the homeless young people aimed for

the Southwest, the Southern Pacific Railroad had serious problems in dealing with these unwanted passengers. During the eight months ending April 30, 1932, officials of that road removed 416,915 men and boys from freight trains and yards. In spite of this precaution, fifty-five were killed and 108 injured. The railroad's special agents were powerless in many towns to operate effectively.

When they walked alongside a freight train that had halted and drove the men and boys out of the cars, the local police would bar the roads leading to the town. It might be fifty miles or more to the next hamlet and the town fathers did not want to have to feed those evicted from the train. Deming, New Mexico, for example, employed a special policeman to keep the wanderers from alighting, while the Southern Pacific agent tried to throw the men off the cars!

Most towns did not welcome strangers. They could not afford to feed visitors, and they wanted to save any available jobs for their own residents. As a result, homeless girls and boys and older men faced an endless ride because no one wanted to feed, help, or employ them. This was young Larry's experience after a week of riding the freights with Tom.

"Everybody out! Hurry it up! Come on, you in the corner there!"

The order was nothing new to Larry, who was now as knowledgeable about the art of hopping freights as a seasoned hobo. He and Tom were somewhere in New Mexico. His clothing was filthy and torn, his face caked with dirt and grease, and only a bath would rid him of the smell. He had not slept in a bed or had a real meal since he left home. The previous night he and Tom had shared some "mulligan" with a group of hoboes camped near the railroad yard. The stew was good, but the little portion of gravy and shreds of meat and vegetables in the bottom of a rusty tin plate was only a taste. However, two cups of weak coffee helped to fill his stomach temporarily. After eating, Larry had slept on the ground by the fire until Tom woke him, so they could catch the early morning westbound freight.

They rode all day until the railroad agent discovered them hiding in the boxcar. Tom had hoped he could somehow slip into California, where he had heard there were jobs picking grapes.

Now, as the boys were walking down the narrow dusty street that led from the railroad into the tiny town, they were pleased to find that no police barred their way. A dozen boys and girls straggled behind.

"There's the Army!" Tom's eyes brightened. "Let's go in!"

They entered a large hall which the Salvation Army used for their meetings. At one end stood a cook stove and a table piled with soup dishes.

"Good evening, fellows," a Salvation Army worker called. "Sign the register, please. Soup?"

The boys hurried forward, wrote their names and addresses in the notebook, and eagerly took the bowls of hot, greasy water. Tom asked where they might find beds for the night.

"Haven't any here," the man replied, "but they can put you up at the jail—that is, if there's room." Just then the girls and boys that had followed Larry and Tom from the train entered the hall. "Better hurry over to the jail," the worker whispered.

"One thing more," Tom said, as he put down his soup bowl. "Any chance of getting a pair of sneakers? I'm going lame." He held out his foot that had the torn sneaker. The toe was gone and half of the sole had worn off.

The man shook his head. "Sorry, but we have clothing only for the people who live here in town. We couldn't begin to take care of those who get off the trains."

"O.K., and thanks anyway." Then the boys hurried down to the tiny jail that was in the cellar of the ancient town hall.

"Come in, boys," the elderly warden called when they appeared at the door. " 'Tain't fancy, but you're welcome to our hospitality for the night. Only got room for you two."

Larry sighed with happiness. At last, he thought, a bed to sleep in, a hot bath and a good night's rest.

A rusty washbasin with cold running water was the closest Larry got to a bath. He washed his face, arms and feet as best he could without soap. He felt ashamed to think of getting into a bed in such a filthy condition, but he quickly discovered that his worry was unnecessary. The bed was a dirty pallet on the floor. There was not even a blanket.

" 'Night, fellers," the warden called. "I'm closing up now. Let you out in the morning."

Larry looked at Tom in astonishment. He had not expected to be locked up like a prisoner.

"Where's the toilet?" Tom called.

"Ain't none. You'll find a bucket in the corner."

In the morning the warden opened the barred door and told them to leave town. "One night's stay is all we allow here."

"Back to the good old S.P.," Tom said bitterly, as they trudged toward the railroad yard. When they reached the station they joined a crowd of some fifty other young people herded behind a fence. A burly railroad policeman stood on the other side of the barricade. Behind him a powerful mountain locomotive was hooking on to a long freight.

"I'm warning you to stay where you are," the officer said.

A few minutes later his words were forgotten when the train started to move slowly. There was a sudden movement in the crowd. Those in front climbed over the fence and were followed by the others. As they stampeded toward the train, the policeman caught two boys but could not stop more. Within two minutes all of these freight hoppers had found places on the train, which was rapidly picking up speed.

Three months later Larry, by now an experienced traveler, arrived in Cleveland. Tom had stayed out in California for the winter, but Larry wanted to return to the East. He reasoned that if he could not go home, he would at least be somewhere nearby and could travel from one large city to another because the authorities usually provided better food and housing than in the country.

Once his money was gone, Larry learned how to beg and forage for himself. He avoided the mission and relief stations in large cities, where welfare workers sometimes tried to send boys home or put them in detention camps. He quickly discovered that in most towns the men who rode the freights got six meals and two nights' lodging but the youths received one meal and a single overnight lodging. Often a meal had to be earned by doing pick-and-shovel work or other menial jobs.

In a few towns food could be obtained by begging at back doors of homes and on the streets. Old women were the best prospects, Larry found. Young married women were sometimes generous, but single women seldom gave him money. On the other hand, Negroes were glad to share what little they had. The hoboes and older men on the march who lived in the "jungles" close to the railroad tracks were usually hospitable. There were also the other "jungles" inhabited by youths who rarely turned away a stranger.

Food was always uppermost in Larry's mind. If he could not find a "jungle" with extra rations to spare, he was compelled to visit a town each day and find the Salvation Army flophouse, a mission, or a municipal welfare station. It was safe to do this in less populated areas, because no effort was made to put tramps to work or send youths home. Most public and private agencies required all recipients of food or shelter to register. Registration served the purpose of keeping records and making certain that a tramp did not overstay his or her welcome. It entitled one to a ticket for a meal, the inevitable bowl of soup or, if the person was fortunate, beans, stew, or a peanut-butter sandwich.

Now, as Larry walked away from the freight yard, a policeman stopped him.

"Hey, boy, where are you going?"

"Soup kitchen," Larry said, hoping that there would be a piece of bread in the watery liquid that often passed for food. He was famished and half frozen. His ten dollars had disappeared some time ago and his clothes were so worn that they gave scant protection from the biting wind.

"Come with me." The policeman led Larry over to a squad car and drove him to the Cleveland Boys Bureau. Here he was directed to a case worker who interviewed him and recorded their conversation.

"I'm going to send you to one of our agencies where they'll give you some clean clothes, a bath, and a hot meal," she said. "You should be at home, not riding endlessly about the country. I'm going to find out if your family can't take you back somehow."

Larry's face reddened. He wanted to return, but he did not want his family to suspect that he could not manage on his own.

"I don't think my father would be pleased to have me come home," he said.

"We'll see about that," the case worker replied. "Meanwhile, you'll get cleaned up and have a nourishing meal. Sound good?"

Larry nodded and smiled. She had no idea how good it sounded!

Two days later he returned to her desk.

"Good news, Larry," the case worker said. "Your family wants you back. Your father has a job. He's been trying to find you for some time."

"Thank you!" He rose from the chair and started to leave. "I'll hit the rails right away."

"Wait a minute. You don't have to ride the rails. Here's a ticket to St. Louis. We want you to travel home safely, and in style!"

Aside from the bread lines, which more often gave bowls of soup or the skimpy meals that charitable agencies provided, until 1933 little was done to help the youths who were on the roads. The Transient Emergency Act granted Federal funds to states that had transient detention camps. These quarters helped to break up the tribes for a time as girls were sent to special homes or returned to their families and boys were assigned to temporary work camps. The more adventurous young people began to shun the camps, however, preferring the freer life of the open road.

The establishment of the Civilian Conservation Corps (CCC) in 1933 provided immediate jobs for many young men. As the PWA and other New Deal alphabet agencies began to erase unemployment and as funds for home relief enabled families to stay together, the number of homeless young people diminished, for in most cases it was no longer necessary to remain on the road or escape to it.

The story of those years when thousands of girl and boy tramps wandered about our nation without adequate food, shelter, or clothing is almost unbelievable. It is difficult to realize the desperation that made parents willing to send young girls and boys from home. It is equally hard to understand how so many communities could have treated the wanderers so heartlessly. But this was a time when there was no money and when there was no Federal aid to help either families or communities.

It is doubtful that such a cruel and shameful episode could occur again in the United States, now that the Federal government stands ready to provide financial assistance for public welfare.

10

DISASTER ON THE FARM

The Devastating Drought

The farmer, shoulders slumped, stood in the center of the field leaning on his hoe. It was August, 1930, and all that was left of the once-green plants was half-grown, withered stalks of corn.

"It's no use, Mary," he said to his wife. "We're done for." He motioned toward the brown pasture. "Cows won't last much longer. Look, you can see their bones now." He kicked at the cementlike dirt which had deep cracks, looked up at the blazing sky, then turned and walked listlessly toward the farmhouse.

There had been more than enough moisture early in the year and most farmers who lived in or near the valleys of the Mississippi, Missouri, Ohio, and Potomac Rivers had looked forward to a good season for their crops. The usual spring rains failed to come, however, and as spring gave way to the hot summer months, no rain clouds appeared over the vast area. In one Kentucky town the temperature soared to 114°, and with no humidity in the air the crops quickly burned and shriveled. Everywhere streams, ponds, wells, and small rivers dried up, and in many areas the only available water was that pumped from deep within the earth. Hydroelectric plants shut down, and many navigable rivers like the Mississippi became so low that it was increasingly dangerous to operate boats on them.

Thousands of farmers had an added daily chore—lugging water for livestock and family. Horse-drawn wagons, trucks, and even railroad trains were pressed into service to supply towns with water. Food for livestock grew scarce, and the railroads voluntarily reduced freight rates for feed shipped to drought areas.

Summer turned into fall, and still there was no rain. Instead, there was an alarming shortage of three hundred billion tons of water! By now the drought-stricken areas extended over twenty-one states, and hundreds of thousands of men, women, and children were its victims. The problem was not one of mass relief, as in 1927 when the Mississippi had overflowed its banks, but a matter of giving assistance to individuals who, although they remained in their homes, were widely scattered and often living in remote inaccessible areas.

By August, the emergency had become so acute that President Hoover called a meeting of the drought state governors and Federal officials. It was decided to coordinate the services of the Red Cross, private credit companies, and Federal agencies through special state and county relief committees. At the same time, the President directed that Federal road and public works programs be set up in drought areas and the Federal Land Bank and the Farm Board expand their credit facilities. The Red Cross, whose Congressional charter charges it with responsibility to provide disaster relief for the nation, appropriated five million dollars for the aid of drought sufferers, a substantial sum inasmuch as the purchasing power of the dollar was roughly twice what it was thirty years later, in 1966.

They called it drought relief, but it was more than that. Before this vicious burning summer heat had laid waste so much farmland, a large part of the South had suffered flood after flood, plus a series of discouraging crop failures and price breaks. Savings were gone, homes were heavily mortgaged, many farmers were deeply in debt, and the price of cotton had dropped from twenty cents a pound to eight cents. Worst of all, the little vegetable gardens on which most families depended for much of their food had produced nothing but dried masses of weeds and stunted, burned plants. There would be little in the larder for the coming winter.

Red Cross Assistance

By October, some 238 counties in Arkansas, Kentucky, Mississippi, and Texas were in such bad trouble that they were receiving aid from the Red Cross. November was not quite so bad, for such cotton as had survived the rainless summer was picked and men found some seasonal work. December brought a new crisis, though. Food and clothing were needed desperately and quickly to meet the cold winter weather. By the first of the New Year

(1931) the Red Cross was reaching 338 counties, or two hundred and twenty-five thousand people, and within thirty days the number jumped to over seven hundred thousand individuals in 663 counties of nineteen states. When early in February two more states were added, Red Cross officials began to wonder where it would end. There was no time to ponder the question, however, for the needs of the present were too pressing.

"We must go to the people," said the Red Cross. "They cannot come to us. We follow roads as long as there are roads. Then we take to pack mules. And always and often there is shank's mare to fall back on. You reach an isolated cabin and find a gaunt family subsisting on corn meal and blue milk. A skeleton cow stares at you. A dead mule lies over in the field. Clothing is in rags. 'No, ma'am, we ain't hungry. We still got half a sack o' meal an' ol' Sukey ain't dry yet. There's folks worse off'n us. Now back yonder in the woods—'

"So we go 'back yonder' and find families sleeping in leaves, huddled together on the floor. Beds and stoves have been sold to the junkman for a few cents. 'Yes'm, we're bad off, but they say there's folk up the crick that's worse.' So up the dry bed of the 'crick' we toil. We don't dare not follow up every report. So often it's true."

Until the first of January, 1931, half of the drought relief came from local Red Cross chapter funds. During January, only 11 per cent was contributed by these same groups, and by February almost all chapter funds were depleted and future help had to come from the national office.

Already Congress had appropriated forty-seven million dollars to finance loans to farmers for the purchase of seed, fertilizer, and feed. Many people wondered why funds were voted only to feed animals and not human beings. So far, President Hoover had relied on the Red Cross to handle the bulk of the relief cases in the drought-stricken area, in order to avoid giving people a government dole. When the Senate tried to appropriate twenty-five million dollars for the Red Cross, the Administration blocked the move. Because it appeared that Congress might vote money for the Red Cross, voluntary givers held back and the drive for funds was not successful, in spite of a well-publicized national campaign. Finally, President Hoover led the Red Cross drive to a successful conclusion, and with the money which was raised the organization administered relief to over two and a half million needy persons during the winter months.

Farmers' Families Hungry, Too!

Meanwhile, in the town of England, Arkansas, because the Red Cross office had temporarily run out of relief application blanks, some five hundred farmers, many of whom were armed, along with their wives stormed into the little business section and demanded food.

George E. Morris, a local attorney, tried to quiet the mob, but it would not let him speak.

"Our children are crying for food and we're going to get it!" a woman shouted.

"We are not going to let our children starve!" cried another.

"We're not beggars! We're willing to work for fifty cents a day, but we're not going to starve and let our families starve," asserted a voice from the rear.

The merchants furnished food to more than three hundred of the men before the crowd quieted down and order was restored.

You saw the same picture in front of the Red Cross office in any one of a thousand communities. There were ragged children, undernourished and blue with cold, who came seeking clothing. There were distraught fathers with large families waiting to receive the disbursing order that meant food for another week. There were frantic mothers begging medical aid for babies dying of malnutrition or other diseases that attack the underfed.

Over in Alabama, many of those who had been evicted as tenant farmers or had lost their jobs took possession of abandoned farms and began to plow the drought-hardened earth, hoping to raise some cotton. They did this in spite of the fact that there was already overproduction and little chance of selling it at a decent price.

Throughout the cotton and tobacco areas the tenant-farmer and sharecropper systems predominated. In those sections where drought had destroyed the main crop, the people were reduced to absolute want and privation as contrasted to those farmers who conducted diversified farming, many of whom were able to save at least one crop from the searing drought.

A Vicious Circle

Everywhere farmers had difficulty reimbursing merchants and banks for the loans which they had taken out early in 1930 to buy seeds, supplies, and food. This was customary practice, because farmers paid off their debts during the summer and fall as they sold their crops and then started their borrowing again in the winter when they ran out of cash. Due to the drought, however, this normal borrowing-repaying cycle was disrupted.

In addition to being unable to make payments on their

mortgages, most farmers could not settle the loans they had obtained from the banks and merchants. Thus the storekeepers were unable to repay what they owed the banks, and the banks, which had tied up all their money in loans to farmers and retailers, were no longer able to lend and many were forced to close. Few farmers were able to get further credit and the relief money appropriated by the Federal government for public works did not help many sharecroppers, tenant or independent farmers. As someone said, "The farmer asked for bread and they gave him a forty-five-million-dollar loan for mule feed, fertilizer, and seed." The outlook was bleak.

Nevertheless, in spite of hunger, privation, and loss, everywhere there was that same philosophy of courage and hope, so typically American. Throughout the drought area men and women were declaring bravely, "If we can just 'get by' until spring, everything will be all right."

"Get by" meant to plant and harvest another crop so that they could weather the coming winter of 1931–1932.

Fortunately, due to the previous abundant years, the nation had such large supplies of food stored away that many people looked on the drought as nature's way of balancing overproduction. However, when the first meager and scattered rains came in the spring of 1931, no one, including the farmer, the relief worker, the politician, and even the meteorologist, knew that these were but token showers.

It seemed as though the fates had conspired against America. The depression was bad enough, but the widespread farm disaster only worsened the over-all economic situation. At a time when the country desperately needed more money in circulation and more buying power to stimulate factory production and general business activity, it was estimated that the farmers' purchasing power was cut by over 12 per cent. Amazingly, in spite of all their troubles during the first year of the drought, farmers repaid 75 per cent of the seed and feed loans, there was little loss of livestock and relief expenditures of the Red Cross totaled less than ten million dollars. No one had starved to death, and in each community Americans had taken care of each other without direct aid from Washington.

Those farmers who optimistically faced the summer of 1931 did not know that the country had already experienced only the first stage of what was to become the worst drought in its history.

President Hoover had tried innumerable ideas to solve the farm problem of low prices and overproduction. In 1929, Congress had authorized the eight-member Federal Farm Board, which encouraged the establishment of farm cooperatives with a half-billion-dollar revolving fund to lend. Mr. Hoover believed that this was a democratic and practical way to solve the problem because the farmers would buy, pack, and sell, working together and achieving many economies. The Federal Farm Board was to buy farm surpluses and hold them until prices in world markets were favorable. Every time that money was used to buy up surplus, however, instead of cutting back production, the farmers only planted more crops and drove prices farther down.

In order to reduce the surpluses, the President recommended that farm lands be withdrawn from cultivation, that young animals be slaughtered, and that crops be plowed under. These radical proposals were not adopted until the advent of the New Deal two years later. In 1932, representatives of leading farm organizations met in Washington to ask for a program that would solve farm surpluses, but nothing came of it. At this point, some farmers decided to take matters into their own hands.

The "Farm Holiday"

The husky, well-tanned men sat around the flickering campfire, their felt hats pulled down over their eyes. The blue denim overalls felt good in the evening damp. It was August, 1932. A few of them were singing a song they had just learned:

"Let's call a Farmers' Holiday,
  A Holiday let's hold;
We'll eat our wheat and ham and eggs
  And let them eat their gold.

"They say the people are with us," one of the pickets observed quietly. "That's all we need. Withholding farm produce is the only way to fight falling farm prices."

"Maybe," drawled another, "but some claim they don't approve of violence, and—"

"It's not violence when you're only protecting your livelihood!" interrupted an angry voice.

In the distance there was the sound of an approaching vehicle.

"Truck!" someone yelled.

The eighteen men jumped to their feet and ran to the nearby highway that led to Sioux City, Iowa. Some carried ax handles and clubs; others stood by the huge planks into which they had driven spikes and which served as a barricade. Four men stood tensely by a telephone pole, ready to roll it onto the road if necessary.

Two headlights cut through the mist and pinpointed the men in their beams. Even before the truck had stopped, some of the picketers had jumped on it to examine its contents.

"It's O.K.," a man called out. "Empty."

The others jumped off and dragged the heavy plank to one side so that the truck could proceed.

A few minutes later another truck approached. This one did not fare so well.

"End of the road for you, mister," one of the pickets told the driver. "Turn around and go back where you came from."

The thin man behind the wheel was shaking with fright. "But it's not my truck. The tomatoes will rot; I'll—"

"Didn't you hear the warning on the radio? We bought radio time to show we meant business. Now turn around or we'll turn your truck over. How would you like that?" He paused for a moment, then added, "What's more, I can get a hundred more men here in a jiffy to help if we need them."

This was but one of many groups of farmers who were picketing the Iowa roads leading into Council Bluffs, Sioux City, Des Moines, and Omaha, Nebraska. They were among the two million members claimed by the National Farm Holiday Association in twenty-four states and headed by a curly-haired and bespectacled farmer, Milo Reno. He asserted that he and his followers would fight for fair prices "until the buying power of the farmer is restored, which can be done only by conceding him the right to cost of production based on an American standard of existence. Business institutions, whether great or small, important or humble, must suffer."

There was picketing in Iowa, Minnesota, and Wisconsin. Near Sioux City, the pickets took a sheriff's badge and gun and threw them into a cornfield. Others seized milk trucks, dumped the milk out on the road, or saved it to distribute free in the city. In Council Bluffs, sixty farmers were arrested, whereupon a thousand of their friends and neighbors marched to the city jail and forced the prisoners' release.

"They call us radicals," Reno said on another occasion. "We're not. All we ask is that the farmers who produce this nation's food shall receive in return the cost of production. Is that radicalism?"

Elsewhere in the country there were milk strikes where dairy farmers overturned trucks, used guns to enforce their demands, stoned buildings, and stopped transportation.

The Problem of Foreclosures

Like all protests, these too came to an end and farmers continued to receive next to nothing for their produce. As a result, their immediate worry was not low prices, but rather the threat of foreclosure. In many communities, vigilante committees threatened to kill insurance agents and bank presidents if they foreclosed certain properties, and on numerous occasions committee members attended sales where they bought back the property at a low price to return it to the unfortunate farmer. Such a group came to the rescue of a farmer in Woodbury County, Iowa.

A crowd of grim-faced men and women had gathered at the home of a tenant farmer where there was to be an auction. They stood resolutely in front of the porch, not to buy bargains for themselves, but to help the tenant farmer who could not pay off a three-hundred-dollar chattel mortgage. The stocky businessman who held the note had obtained the legal right to auction everything the family owned in order to raise his three hundred dollars. Now, as he stood on the steps about to start the sale, he felt uneasy. All the men and women facing him had hatred in their eyes.

"Sid, step over here a minute," a big farmer whispered to a friend.

"Yes?"

"We don't want any trouble. He might get ideas of calling the sheriff." He nodded slightly in the direction of the shed behind the house. "Take your pliers and sort of walk over there and cut those telephone wires."

As soon as the sale began it was apparent that things would go for a few cents apiece instead of dollars. At last, when everything had gone, the total sum of $11.75 had been realized. Someone took up a collection to buy the items back for the farmer while the leader of the group gently persuaded the fat creditor to sign a quit claim which would discharge the debt forever.

Near Oklahoma City, eight farmers were arrested for obstructing the foreclosure of a mortgage on a farm owned by a man of seventy. In LeMars, Iowa, six hundred farmers pulled a foreclosing judge from his chambers and nearly killed him. At Pringhar, Iowa, farmers who were leading a riot forced the local sheriff to kneel down and kiss the flag. Like the farmers who closed roads during the "Farm Holiday," these men saw nothing wrong in taking the law into their own hands. They believed that they had to come to the aid of friends and neighbors who were in danger of losing their homes.

As the number of foreclosures grew, it was evident that something had to be done. In North Dakota, the forced sales of farms was prohibited. During February, 1933, radical farmers threatened to march on the Minnesota state capital if a debt moratorium was not declared. Thereupon the legislature forbade foreclosures for two years.

Shortly after President Roosevelt's inauguration, the Farm Holiday Association met in Des Moines and issued an ultimatum to the new administration: Unless the government met its demands for farm relief by May 3, 1933, the Association would call a nation-wide farmers' strike.

New Deal for the Farmer

"You mean the government wants me to plow that cotton under the ground?" George Pace, a raw-boned Alabama farmer, stared incredulously at his visitor.

"That's right," the eager young man said. He was one of the army of AAA agents who were visiting farmers. "It's the only way to push up prices. That's why Congress adopted the Agricultural Adjustment Act."

The farmer shook his head sadly. "Sounds downright immoral to me, son. It's wrong to destroy, especially when some folks haven't enough to eat. Beside, even though cotton doesn't bring much money, I have to eat, too."

"That's true," the agent agreed, "and the government is ready to pay you if you'll plow the crop under. We'll give you a contract that will pay you benefits for not growing cotton."

Mr. Pace's eyes narrowed. "You mean you'll pay me for *not* growing?"

The agent nodded and smiled.

"Well! I never!"

Obviously Mr. Pace had not been reading the newspapers. Otherwise, he would have learned that twelve days after his inauguration President Roosevelt sent a farm relief message to Congress. He asked for power to reduce acreage in certain crops before spring planting and for credit relief to save farmers in immediate danger of losing their homes.

"I tell you," he said, "that it is a new and untrod path, but I tell you with equal frankness than an unprecedented condition calls for the trial of new means to rescue agriculture."

There began then what columnist Walter Lippmann described as "the most daring economic experiment ever seriously proposed in the United States."

Things happened quickly:

1. On May 12, 1933, the Agricultural Adjustment Act (AAA) became law. Designed to raise farm prices by buying up crops and livestock of farmers who limited their acreage, it was financed by a processing tax levied on commodities and paid by the consumer.
2. On the same date the Emergency Farm Mortgage Act authorized emergency loans to help farmers in danger of foreclosure.
3. The Farm Credit Act of June 16, 1933, provided short-term loans to farmers and livestock producers who needed cash.

By August, ten million acres of cotton had been plowed under and by September two hundred and twenty thousand young sows and six million pigs had been slaughtered, all at the cost of a hundred million dollars. Henry Wallace, Secretary of Agriculture, who was a farmer himself, was as loath as anyone to do this, but limitation of farm production seemed to be the only answer.

In 1935, farm incomes were almost double those of 1933 and for the first time the farmer felt that the government was really helping him. This miracle was cut short in January, 1935, when the Supreme Court declared the AAA unconstitutional. The court's action did not discourage Congress, however. Under the guise of conservation, it legislated a new AAA in 1938 as well as other legislation to benefit the farmers.

Probably the most significant fact about the first AAA program was that the urban majority in Congress recognized that a prosperous nation depended on a healthy agricultural community. Furthermore, these legislators were willing to subsidize the farmer by taxing consumers and the nation at large so as to channel a portion of the national wealth to the farming minority. Paying farmers for what they did not grow thus became the government's permanent policy.

11

LABOR AND THE NEW DEAL

"If You Don't Like It, Quit!"

The woman returned home from the Hudson Motor Company plant weary and discouraged.

"Second day I sat there from eight until four." She slumped into the old chair by the big wood stove. "Why did they call me in if they had no work?" She had spent twenty cents each day for carfare—money she could not afford to waste.

"What did they tell you today?" her husband asked. He had not worked for several months.

"Come back tomorrow." She shook her head. "I'll do it once more. We can't afford to spend twenty cents a day for nothing."

The next evening she came home at the same time and dropped a quarter and three pennies on the kitchen table.

"That's what I made today. A half hour's work! Twenty-eight cents pay for three days in that plant, and I spent sixty cents for carfare. 'No more work,' the man said. No wonder we need a union!"

So many unemployed men and women were looking for jobs that some automobile manufacturers and other industrialists were able to shift their operations to piece rates instead of hourly wages. Thus, if the employee could not work because the machine broke or poor management planning left him idle, he, not the employer, was the loser.

In the Midwest, an unemployed factory worker answered an advertisement.

"Must be forty of us here applying for this one job," he commented to the man standing beside him.

"And what chance does a man have?" the other asked. "How can any employer know who to pick?"

At that moment the boss came into the hall and studied the eager strained faces before him. Finally he pointed to a tall strapping workman standing in front.

"You can have the job. I'll pay you fifteen dollars a week."

Immediately a small thin man shot his hand into the air. "I'll take the job for ten dollars," he shouted.

The boss smiled and shrugged his shoulders. "O.K., it's yours. Step inside."

It was easy for employers to ignore and even violate such labor laws as then existed. An employer in Allentown, Pennsylvania, was fined one hundred dollars for making children work fifty to a hundred hours a week and failing to carry workmen's compensation. Later it was discovered that he subsequently withheld twenty-two cents from the pay of each child in order to pay the fine. In another Pennsylvania sweatshop the children under sixteen went out on strike because half of them were earning less than $7.40 a week.

"If you don't like it, quit! I can get plenty of others to work," was the usual heartless answer employers gave to those who protested.

The Negro worker had an even harder time. Negroes were not employed in offices, and few government jobs were open to them. Unable to obtain decent education, not many had any skills to offer and most unions rebuffed them. From time to time Negroes had been lured to the North as strikebreakers when unskilled workers were needed to replace white men on strike. Even though the Communists forced many unions to admit Negroes as members, that did not guarantee them jobs. Previously there had been "white jobs" and "nigger jobs," but during the depression the white men took the latter.

Decline of the Labor Movement

Labor and management have been in conflict since the founding of our nation. It took years for labor to win the eight-hour day in some industries, to stamp out child labor in various states, and to stop the exploitation of women in certain businesses. Nevertheless, in spite of the progress that had been achieved, many of the old evils still existed at the start of the depression.

During the nineteen-twenties, the labor movement suffered a decline and union membership dropped. Businessmen, bankers, farm leaders, and others backed a new movement which they called the "American Plan." This held that it was the right and privilege of every American to enter any business or trade he chose, and to make an agreement with an employer without interference from a union agent. The "American Plan" sought to reestablish company unions or open shops—where nonunion labor could be hired—by bringing back the "yellow dog" contracts which prohibited employees from joining labor unions. Trade-union leaders naturally wanted the closed shops, where only union members could be employed.

At the same time that the open shop was returning, the labor movement suffered several setbacks on the legal front as Federal courts voided many of the legislative gains workingmen had won during the progressive period prior to the war. The use of court injunctions became common, and one of them, in the Red Jacket Coal Company case, went so far as to forbid all attempts to organize coal miners.

In 1930, there was a change in this anti-union attitude. The Supreme Court handed down a surprising decision which had the effect of sanctioning unionism. That same year the United States Senate refused to confirm the appointment of Circuit Judge John J. Parker to the Supreme Court partly because of his decision approving a "yellow dog" contract in the Red Jacket case. Two years later, the Norris-LaGuardia Act limited the power of Federal courts to use injunctions in labor disputes and forbade "yellow dog" contracts.

Nevertheless, many companies made certain that their employees did not join unions. In 1934, the La Follette Civil Liberties Committee listed some twenty-five hundred companies which previously had been found using detective agencies to fight unions. Some automobile manufacturers hired company spies to report on union activities, and any men caught joining a union or urging other employees to sign up were fired quickly. Managements stooped to almost any practice in order to intimidate their employees. This explains the success of a professional strikebreaking company like Bergoff, Inc. It described its services as follows:

The Strike Prevention Department. This department is composed of men possessing natural leadership qualifications. Men of intelligence, men of great persuasive powers, to counteract the evil influence of agitators and the radical element.

The Undercover Department. Our undercover department is composed of carefully selected male and female mechanics and workpeople. They furnish accurate information on the movements and contemplated actions of their fellow employees—"forewarned is forearmed."

The Open-Shop Department. This department is composed of an organization equipped to supply all classes of competent mechanics and workpeople to keep the wheels of industry moving during a strike.

The Protection Department. This department is composed of big, disciplined men with military or police experience, for the protection of life and property.

The Investigation Department. Our investigation department is international in scope and embraces all branches. The personnel is composed of male and female operators of the highest caliber.

This was part of the labor picture when the New Deal came into power. The other part was the ugly fact that approximately fifteen million men and women could not find work.

The Blue Eagle

Those who could not get downtown to line the streets heard the NRA parade described on their radios as city after city celebrated the birth of the Blue Eagle and, hopefully, the nation's return to prosperity.

Again New Yorkers, on September 13, 1933, led the way with the biggest, the most elaborate, and probably the most musical parade. More than a quarter of a million people, both labor and management, were there. They were organized in seventy-seven industry and trade divisions led by the music of hundreds of bands while airplanes zoomed overhead. A million and a half New Yorkers lined both sides of Fifth Avenue for four miles to help celebrate the great event.

There were clerks and office boys, bankers and salesmen. Paramount Theater girls, dressed like blue eagles, marched beside young members of the new Civilian Conservation Corps, who wore natty olive uniforms. Dressmakers and waitresses strode ahead of brewers, mechanics, and municipal workers. Each group marched snappily by the reviewing stand, their banners proclaiming pride in their occupation and faith in America. Everyone wanted to show President Roosevelt and the nation that he was squarely behind the NRA (National Recovery Administration), whose symbol was the Blue Eagle.*

Here, at last, was proof that government could do something. President Roosevelt had promised on that gray March day that "nobody is going to starve." Now, just six months later, the whole country was involved in a

* The National Industrial Recovery Act (NIRA) was the law which provided for establishment of the National Recovery Administration (NRA).

concerted effort that promised to restore confidence and economic well-being to the country.

"We must lay hold of the fact that economic laws are not made by nature," President Roosevelt said. "They are made by men."

The NRA overturned one of the foundation stones of our free enterprise system because it forbade cutthroat competition and overproduction by providing for "self-regulation." Under the law, each industry was to formulate and adopt its own code of practice, which was to be drawn up by a committee representing labor, management, and the public. Every company that signed the code, obligating it to live up to the promises, received a Blue Eagle emblem to display in its place of business.

General Hugh S. Johnson, Administrator of the NRA, found that all businessmen did not share his enthusiasm for the new regulated economy which also required payment of a minimum wage for reasonable hours of work. He had to lock some of the representatives of labor and management in rooms and appeal to their patriotism in order to win agreement. When the oil industry could not decide on a code, Johnson drew one up himself. He was everywhere—urging, threatening, cajoling—until most industries had agreed on their codes.

SECTION 7(A) OF THE NIRA

One reason why many businessmen were not in favor of the NRA was because Section 7(a) of the law (National Industrial Recovery Act) which Johnson wrote, stipulated that:

> Employees shall have the right to organize and bargain collectively through representatives of their own choosing,

and shall be free from the interference, restraint, or coercion of employers of labor, or their agents, in the designation of such representatives.

"Forget about injunctions, blacklists, and the fear of dismissal!" fiery John L. Lewis told his miners. He even had special signs printed and posted by mine entrances. They read:

THE PRESIDENT WANTS YOU TO ORGANIZE!

Coal and steel companies would not sign until forced to do so. Secretary of Labor Frances Perkins asked the presidents of the large steel companies to meet with her so that they might make a joint statement with a labor representative about the wages and hours of the NRA steel code. Miss Perkins later reported that the industrialists retreated "like a bunch of eleven-year-old boys at their first party" at the prospect of having to meet with the president of the American Federation of Labor, William Green. They evidently feared that such a meeting would give the impression that they were in favor of unionization of their plants.

Henry Ford, who was against the principle of the NRA, refused to sign because many of the companies from which he purchased parts were not under codes. Other companies decided to resist unionization, defy the law, and take their cases to the courts. This encouraged labor unions to voice their demands, since the law was on their side and they were ready to use their only real weapon, the strike.

The W. J. Rainey Company of Uniontown, Pennsylvania, suffered the first work stoppage after it discharged two members of workmen's representation committees.

Soon milk producers who received one and a half cents for a quart of milk were fighting state troopers, and tool and die workers in Detroit and miners in Illinois were on strike. Shipyard workers, steelworkers, boot and shoe makers, and even airline pilots struck to enforce their requests for higher pay.

Perhaps it was a bit naïve of the government to expect all businessmen to reverse their long-standing attitude regarding labor. As previously noted, the "American Plan" had proclaimed the sanctity of the open shop and given many employers a sense of security against danger from union organizing. Most industrialists were willing to cooperate with the new President—on their terms—and they never envisioned having union recognition and collective bargaining forced on them.

By August, 1933, there had been a thousand strikes, many caused by disagreements over NRA codes. The most spectacular occurred in San Francisco during July, when a dispute between longshoremen and their employers triggered a general walkout of all workingmen employed by industry and service companies. This paralyzed the entire city for a day. The revolt suddenly collapsed with the arrival of General Johnson, who quickly got in touch with the strike leaders and won their promise to settle their differences peacefully.

A month later, the largest strike in the nation's history erupted in the South and soon spread to some twenty states.

The Textile Strike

"About time for the folks to get out of work." The grizzled old man was sunning himself on the porch steps of the dilapidated house across the road from a typical Southern textile mill. The change of shifts at 3:30 P.M. was the high point of the day for him and his one-armed companion.

He glanced up the road and came to life. "Josh, look up! There's a storm coming!"

"Not a storm," the other contradicted. "That's cars. Looks like one of those flying squadrons we heard about, those fellers trying to organize the mills. You can look for trouble if it is."

A moment later fourteen cars skidded to a sudden noisy stop in front of the mill. They had scarcely halted before some seventy-five men emerged and quickly formed a line. They carried signs, a few of which told workers to quit their jobs; others urged them to join the Textile Workers Union; and some encouraged the mill hands to strike for higher wages and shorter hours.

As the textile workers came out of the plant, the pickets began to march in a circle while their leaders shouted epithets about mill managers and invited the men to join the union. Meanwhile, the factory owner who had seen the flying squadron arrive called the town's one policeman. As soon as the officer reached the scene, the leader of the pickets blew a short blast on a whistle and the men bolted for their cars, jumped inside, and the automobiles roared away. The policeman, the two old men, and a few workers were left to choke on the dust.

"You get their license numbers?" the policeman asked the old-timers.

"What good would that do?" one of them asked. "They was from out of state."

This was one of the many motorcades of pickets that roamed the South. They would appear briefly at a plant, then disappear and show up in another town. Some of them stoned and raided mills, others set fire to property. Six pickets were killed in a clash with sheriff's deputies at Honea Path, South Carolina. Every day the picture changed as a factory would reopen in one hamlet while pickets shut another a few miles away.

It was not difficult for the union to excite workers to rebel. Because the textile industry had been losing money for years, in many areas employers paid low wages but required long working hours. Apparently representatives of the cotton garment industry who met on April 27, 1934, felt that the industry's condition justified adopting a resolution that defied a recent order of President Roosevelt increasing the wages and reducing the hours of work of a quarter of a million employees in forty-two states. The statement defying the President's order called it "unjustifiable, unwarranted, burdensome, and inequitable."

The officers of the textile union decided that they had no alternative but to call a million workers in the cotton, silk, and wool industries out on strike. They felt that the fact that companies had been losing money was no excuse to deny their employees the same social gains that labor was beginning to realize in other industries, thanks to the NRA. Recognition of the union, abolition of the stretch-out and speed-up, a thirty-hour work week, and no reduction in the minimum fourteen-dollar-a-week wage were the union's principal demands.

Most workers were willing to leave their jobs.

"What have we got to lose?" one man asked, as he walked slowly on the picket line in front of the mill where he worked.

"I haven't made a decent week's wages for over six years," the woman ahead of him called over her shoulder.

The strike spread with alarming rapidity. In Massachusetts, a hundred and ten thousand left their machines. Rhode Island counted fifty thousand idle workers. Down in Georgia, sixty thousand stayed away from the factories, while twenty-eight thousand did the same in Alabama. Altogether, half a million men and women refused to work, and there was danger that workers in other industries would also go out in sympathy strikes. It was the most extensive work stoppage our nation had ever suffered.

In a short time the situation became tense. Although the governors of eight states called up the National Guard to keep order, guardsmen and mobs clashed in many places and over twenty persons were killed. Rhode Island's Governor Francis Green summoned the legislature into extraordinary session. He asked the lawmakers to request Federal troops to help the National Guardsmen already on duty patroling the streets.

"We are face to face now not with a textile strike," the Governor warned the legislators, "but with a Communist uprising."

The Senators backed the Governor, but not the members of the House. Many of them were so familiar with conditions in the local mills that they did not believe the Communists were responsible for the strike or that the state was faced with a dire emergency. After talking with President Roosevelt, Governor Green agreed that the situation was not so serious that it required Federal troops.

Shortly thereafter, the President appointed a committee headed by Governor John Winant of New Hampshire to study the situation and make recommendations for its solution. On September 28th, the textile union's executive committee agreed to call off the strike while the Winant Committee met, but when eighty thousand workers in the South returned to their jobs they found some two hundred mills shut. Many textile workers in the Northeast were told that their jobs had been eliminated and some were discriminated against in other ways. It was clear that the mill owners were not prepared to grant any benefits to the strikers.

Twelve days after the union had canceled the strike, Governor Winant made public his committee's "peace treaty," which contained recommendations for improvements in wages, hours, and working conditions. The members of the committee were hopeful that their suggestions would prove acceptable to management and labor. However, since the report was merely advisory and not enforceable, the employees could only hope that some enlightened employers would adopt its provisions or that the government would legislate the suggested improvements.

In most mills, nothing happened. All the strikers had to show for their efforts were three weeks without pay and in many instances lost jobs. The several hundred thousand workers who had joined the United Textile Union during the strike quickly dropped out, disgusted and unable to pay the dues.

This was one case where the NRA had failed to help an industry.

Black Monday

It was Monday morning, May 27, 1935, when the nine judges assembled in their robing room and then one by one slowly and quietly filed into the public hearing room where anxious reporters and government officials had gathered. Tall, distinguished-looking Chief Justice Hughes led the way. The other justices followed, then sat to his right and left according to their seniority. Justice Benjamin N. Cardozo, the youngest member, was on the far end.

Everyone in the courtroom was tense as the decisions were read. The first held that the Chief Executive could not remove members of independent government agencies except for causes specified by Congress. The second declared the Fraser-Lemke Farm Mortgage Moratorium Law was invalid. The third, called the "sick chicken case," threatened the future of the entire New Deal.

A New York City poultry dealer, Joseph Schechter, was accused of violating his NRA code by selling a sick chicken to a butcher. He fought the case up to the Supreme Court to see whether or not the NRA had jurisdiction over his business. Chief Justice Hughes prepared the opinion which not only invalidated the National Industrial Relations Act but also raised questions about the entire New Deal program.

On that "Black Monday" over 750 NRA codes became illegal. The codes in each state and city had their own administrative organizations and tens of thousands of Federal employees were suddenly jobless. Many industrialists quickly abandoned the codes and prepared to attack every New Deal law and regulation that prevented business from operating according to its traditional laissez-faire policy.

The Wagner Act

In 1934, Senator Robert Wagner introduced a bill which clarified and tightened the provisions of the NIRA's Section 7(a). He withdrew his proposal at the request of President Roosevelt, who wanted to give the NRA a

longer trial. By 1935 it became evident that the NIRA
was not achieving its purpose and Senator Wagner therefore reintroduced his bill. The Senate passed it eleven
days before the Supreme Court doomed the NIRA.
When the legislation was sent to the House of Representatives, President William Green of the American Federation of Labor testified before a congressional committee:

> I do not mind telling you, that the spirit of the workers
> in America has been aroused. They are going to find a way
> to bargain collectively. . . . We cannot and will not con-
> tinue to urge workers to have patience unless the Wagner
> bill is made law, and unless it is enforced, once it becomes
> law.

The House of Representatives passed the Wagner Act
and it became law on July 5, 1935.

Henceforth the new National Labor Relations Board
could force employers to obey the law; employers could
not interfere with employees as they exercised guaranteed
rights; employees could not be blacklisted or fined for
union activities; and there could be no discrimination if
workers brought charges against a company.

Often referred to as the cornerstone of the New Deal's
labor program, the Wagner Act made it possible for men
and women to join labor unions without fear of employer
retaliation. Just as important, it permitted unions to sign
up members and represent them aggressively at the bargaining table.

The newly legislated rights were not to be achieved
without a struggle, however. Some industrialists, especially
those heading automobile and steel companies, were still
not ready to bow to union demands, and it took many
strikes and some violence to win full compliance with the

law. Furthermore, there were many who refused to obey the law because they believed that the Supreme Court would find it as unconstitutional as the NIRA.

Two years after passage of the Wagner Act, the Supreme Court, which often reflects public opinion, upheld the Congress' authority to regulate labor conditions. In *N.L.R.B. v. Jones and Laughlin*, Chief Justice Hughes wrote:

> Employees have as clear a right to organize and select their representatives for lawful purposes, as the respondent has to organize its business and select its own officers and agents. Discrimination and coercion to prevent the free exercise of the right of employees to self-organization and representation is a proper subject for condemnation by competent legislative authority.

Nevertheless, it was not until 1941 that the Ford Motor Company, one of the last and largest holdouts, signed a contract with the United Auto Workers which the union praised as "a model for the industry." Collective bargaining, whereby employees are represented by a union of their own choosing, was at last a part of the American way of life.

PART III

Three Decades Later

Now, thirty years after the depression, although the United States has never enjoyed greater prosperity than in the years between, a third of all families are classified as underprivileged. Millions are still living in city slums and substandard housing in rural areas. Unemployment stands at over 5 per cent of the work force, with hundreds of thousands of unskilled workers unable to find jobs. Large numbers of people are receiving welfare checks and farm production is just being freed of controls.

What happened to the social gains achieved during the depression years? Were the privations, the cruel unemployment, and the other hardships endured for naught, or did they help make America a better place in which to live?

This final chapter summarizes some of the ways that the depression years influenced and improved our nation's economic and social life.

12

OUR DEBT TO THE DEPRESSION

ARIZONA SEIZES SAVINGS AGENCY—GIBRALTAR ASSOCIATION
THIRD THRIFT UNIT TO FAIL IN LITTLE MORE THAN MONTH

MARKET SUFFERS A SHARP SETBACK—STOCKS APPEARED
LOW FOR YEAR IN THEIR STEEPEST DECLINE THIS MONTH.

DROUGHT AND SEARING HEAT IN MUCH OF COUNTRY PARCH
PASTURES, REDUCE FARMERS' CROPS

JOHNSON OPENS CAMPAIGN TO FIND JOBS FOR YOUTHS

These headlines, taken from newspapers of the nineteen-sixties, not the nineteen-thirties, would seem to bear out the truth of the French saying, "The more things change the more they are the same." Perhaps they point up the fact that some problem areas are never solved permanently but must be dealt with by each succeeding generation.

No More Bank Holidays

Figures published by the Federal Reserve System on bank suspensions showed that in 1933 exactly 4,004 institutions with deposits of over three and a half billion dollars closed or were placed in receivership. Thanks to the Banking Act of 1933, which prevented banks from using resources of the Federal Reserve System for speculation, and to other improvements made in our banking system during the depression years, the number of bank failures since 1940 has been negligible. In 1945, 1946, and 1948 there were no closings, and the years 1960 and 1962 were low years with two suspensions each.

Because the depression was responsible for more than nine thousand bank failures, money entrusted to banks is now protected by Federal deposit insurance. Even though banks occasionally close, depositors lose nothing if their deposits do not exceed the maximum amount insured by the Federal Deposit Insurance Corporation. Thus the only people to suffer are those who own shares of bank stock, but all stock ownership involves a degree of risk.

Down on the Farm

A well-dressed middle-aged farmer stood by a field in North Dakota. It was the fall of 1964.

"Every four years they come a-courtin'," he said. "Heaven only knows why. We're not as influential as we once were, although we could be if we'd get together.

Our numbers don't make for power any more except for a few close elections here and there."

He was referring to the forthcoming 1964 Presidential election, when both Democratic and Republican nominees would be seeking his vote, and, secondly, to the drastic reduction in the number of farms and farm workers since the depression.

In spite of the exodus of farm workers to the cities, the agricultural output has steadily grown as a result of better fertilizers, the introduction of scientific farming methods, and widespread mechanization.

In 1964, drought, the farmers' old enemy, had caused twelve states to be designated "disaster areas," while in the South the size of the cotton crop was increasing over that of the previous year. Surpluses of many farm commodities were still plaguing the country, but they did not trouble farmers. Since the depression, when the New Deal instituted the system of purchasing surplus crops to maintain prices and the paying of farmers for not planting, Federal payments to farmers in the nineteen-sixties were running well over a billion dollars a year.

Nevertheless, in 1964 there were pockets of trouble. Reminiscent of the farmers' strikes of 1932, the National Farmers Organization was urging its members to withhold crops and cattle from the market in an effort to obtain contracts for higher prices from processors. Violence broke out as once again friend was pitted against friend and neighbor against neighbor. Two pickets died when they tried to prevent a truck from delivering cattle to a stockyard at Bonduel, Wisconsin. The men had climbed onto the vehicle and were rocking it as it passed through a crowd of angry farmers. They lost their grip, fell off, and were run over.

Plantings of the next year's wheat began in mid-August

with the prospect that wheat production would climb during 1965 and further complicate the government's surplus problem even though the United States was beginning to export more wheat abroad.

Three years later the picture had changed. Now there was too much storage space and not enough grain. Instead of storing surplus wheat, the government had surplus metal grain bins. The United States was sending large amounts of bread grains and feed abroad, as people in many countries began to need more food. The world had finally accepted a grim and frightening fact: millions of men, women and children faced certain starvation unless drastic steps were taken to produce more and more food.

It looked as though the problems of overproduction and farm surpluses which had plagued our nation and our farmers since the early nineteen-twenties were definitely past.

"We must recognize that the long road of surplus has had its turning," Vice President Humphrey told a farmers' convention in the summer of 1966. "Next year will be a year for bringing a substantial part of reserve acreage out of mothballs."

More land would have to go back into production and farmers would have to produce as never before to feed a hungry world.

The Poor Amid Prosperity

"Next month? I don't know. It's in the hands of the angels," a Detroit housewife declared, as she tried to support her unemployed husband and five children on a wage of sixty dollars a week.

"Why do we have to go naked and hungry?" asked a distraught Negro mother living in a Chicago slum.

During a time of unparalleled prosperity, the Johnson administration discovered that some thirty-five million Americans, a fifth of our nation, were classified as poor. These were families living on incomes of less than three thousand dollars a year, while mounting inflation was gradually eroding the little buying power that they had.

The "War on Poverty" waged during the nineteen-sixties was trying to give every American a decent standard of living. This was not easy to attain in view of the ever-growing relief army. Between 1954 and 1964, although the populace had grown by 18 per cent, the number of people on relief had increased 42 per cent and was costing taxpayers fifty million dollars a month. During the same time, aid-to-dependent-children (ADC) soared 104 per cent. This was caused partly by unemployment among unskilled workers made idle by automation and partly by the large rise in the number of illegitimate children.

"No one shall starve," President Roosevelt had promised, but neither he nor anyone else could have foreseen just how far this promise would lead. During the depression families stuck together and helped one another, especially aged parents who had nowhere else to turn. Obligation to care for one's elderly parents had been a time-honored tradition, but in 1966 it was declared old-fashioned. That year provisions in Title 19 of the Federal Government's Medicare program eliminated the requirement that children be responsible for their parents' medical bills. In New York State the legislature extended this exemption to support of any kind.

During the same year, a hundred people undertook a "Walk for Decent Welfare," a 155-mile march to the

Ohio state capital, to demand increases in relief payments. Meanwhile, in Washington, D. C., Dr. George A. Wiley, director of the Poverty Action Center, announced that his group would organize the poor so that they would be a more powerful force and could bargain collectively with welfare officials.

On the other hand, members of the government-sponsored VISTA (Volunteers in Service to America), doubtless inspired by the original Civilian Conservation Corps, were undertaking various projects to help poor families throughout the nation. At the same time, many church-sponsored groups of young people, and others not connected with any church, were going out to meet and work with the underprivileged and poor.

The spirit of Americans helping Americans was not dead after all!

Gains for Labor

In 1933, the worst year of the depression, a quarter of our civilian labor force was unemployed. Thirty years later, during a time of great prosperity, almost five million men and women were jobless. In some industries automation had created unemployment, the need for further training had idled others, especially the unskilled. It was evident that there would always be some people who could or would not work.

The depression years bequeathed to the American worker two invaluable rights:

1. Unemployment insurance, which provides some financial aid while one is out of work; and
2. The legal right to form and belong to unions when desir-

able or necessary in order to obtain decent working conditions.

Gains which labor unions made during the depression were matched later by equally important legislation which sought to guarantee equal pay for equal work and abolish discrimination in hiring.

Few people during the depression years believed that the government "owed" them a job or a regular wage. They sought opportunity to work and felt that if private business could not provide jobs that the government should take steps to stimulate business or provide public works projects which in turn would give direct employment. No one was "owed" a job, however.

Nevertheless, the depression, with its massive appropriations for relief and public works projects, paved the way for the philosophy of "let the government take care of you." Disturbed by this trend, President Kennedy once urged every American to "Ask not what your country can do for you—ask what you can do for your country."

No More Depressions?

Perhaps the most important lesson we learned from the depression of the nineteen-thirties was how to prevent another such catastrophe. As a result, the term *depression*, familiar only to those who lived through it, has been replaced by the word recession, which the dictionary defines as "a slight depression."

Today we know how to manipulate our economy by regulating the supply of money and by raising or lowering personal and corporate income taxes. Government spending for public works and other projects can provide employment quickly and stimulate business if needed.

The depression was tragic, but, unlike many of history's disasters from which mankind has learned little or nothing, our nation profited by this experience. Not only do we enjoy revolutionary social changes but in the future, if our economy suffers further "recessions," it is unlikely that any administration will stand by and permit another depression like that of the nineteen-thirties to develop.

Suggested Readings

ALLEN, FREDERICK LEWIS: *The Big Change*, Harper & Brothers, New York, 1952.

——: *Since Yesterday*, Harper & Brothers, New York, 1939.

ALLEN, ROBERT S.: *Why Hoover Faces Defeat*, Brewer, Warren and Putnam, New York, 1932.

BEALS, CARLETON: *The Story of Huey P. Long*, J. B. Lippincott Co., Philadelphia, 1935.

BIRD, CAROLINE: *The Invisible Scar*, David McKay Company, Inc., New York, 1966.

BLUM, JOHN MORTON: *From the Morgenthau Diaries, Years of Crisis, 1928–1938*, Houghton Mifflin Co., Boston, 1959.

BROGAN, D. W.: *The Era of Franklin D. Roosevelt*, Yale University Press, New Haven, Conn., 1950.

CHARLES, SEARLE F.: *Minister of Relief: Harry Hopkins and the Depression*, Syracuse University Press, Syracuse, N. Y., 1963.

COREY, HERBERT: *The Truth About Hoover*, Houghton Mifflin Co., Boston, 1932.

DAYTON, ELDOROUS L.: *Walter Reuther, Autocrat of the Bargaining Table*, Devin-Adair Co., New York, 1958.

EINAUDI, MARIO: *The Roosevelt Revolution*, Harcourt, Brace and Co., New York, 1959.

EMERSON, EDWIN: *Hoover and His Times*, Garden City Publishing Co., Garden City, N. Y., 1932.

Five Years of Rural Relief, WPA Division of Social Research, Washington, D. C., 1938.

FLYNN, JOHN T.: *The Roosevelt Myth*, Devin-Adair Co., New York, 1956.

FUSFIELD, DANIEL R.: *The Economic Thought of F.D.R. and the Origins of the New Deal*, Columbia University Press, New York, 1956.

GALBRAITH, JOHN KENNETH: *The Great Crash, 1929*, Princeton University Press, Princeton, N. J., 1963.

HOOVER, HERBERT: *Memoirs* (3 volumes), The Macmillan Co., New York, 1951.

HOPKINS, HARRY L.: *Spending to Save*, W. W. Norton and Co., New York, 1936.

HOYT, EDWIN P.: *The Tempering Years*, Charles Scribner's Sons, New York, 1963.

ICKES, HAROLD: *The Secret Diary of Harold L. Ickes*, Simon and Schuster, Inc., New York, 1954.

JONES, JESSE H., with EDWARD ANGLY: *Fifty Billion Dollars: My Thirteen Years with the RFC*, The Macmillan Company, New York, 1951.

LAWRENCE, DAVID: *Nine Honest Men*, D. Appleton-Century Co., New York, 1936.

LINK, ARTHUR S.: *American Epoch, A History of the United States Since the 1890's*, Alfred A. Knopf, Inc., New York, 1962. (See Chapters 14–20.)

LORD, RUSSELL: *The Wallaces of Iowa*, Houghton Mifflin Co., Boston, 1947.

MOLEY, RAYMOND: *After Seven Years*, Harper & Brothers, New York, 1939.

PATTERSON, ROBERT T.: *The Great Boom and Panic*, Henry Regnery Company, Chicago, 1965.

PERKINS, DEXTER: *The New Age of Franklin Roosevelt*, University of Chicago Press, Chicago, 1957.

RAUCH, BASIL: *The History of the New Deal*, Creative Age Press, Inc., New York, 1944.

ROOSEVELT, ELEANOR: *This Is My Story*, Harper & Brothers, New York, 1949.

ROOSEVELT, FRANKLIN D.: *F.D.R.–His Personal Letters* (4 volumes), Duell, Sloan and Pearce, New York, 1947.

SCHLESINGER, ARTHUR M., JR.: *The Coming of the New Deal*, Houghton Mifflin Company, Boston, 1959.

SHANNON, DAVID A., ED.: *The Great Depression*, Prentice-Hall, Inc., Englewood Cliffs, N. J., 1960.

SHERWIN, MARK, and MARKMANN, CHARLES LAM: *One Week in March*, G. P. Putnam's Sons, New York, 1961.

WARREN, HARRIS GAYLORD: *Herbert Hoover and the Great Depression*, Oxford University Press, New York, 1959.

WISH, HARVEY: *Contemporary America, the National Scene Since 1900*, Harper & Brothers, New York, 1955. (See Chapters 15–19.)

INDEX

About the Author

Adrian A. Paradis, the author of more than twenty books for young readers, was born in 1912 in the first apartment house in Brooklyn, New York, to have an elevator. He entered Dartmouth College in 1930 and at that time hoped to go to the Yale School of Drama after graduating from college. The Depression, the subject of *The Hungry Years*, changed his plans and, after several jobs paying little money, he entered the hotel business with a friend. While managing a small inn up in the White Mountains of New Hampshire, he met his future wife, and soon afterward left the hotel business.

He next studied library service at Columbia University at night, while he worked in a law library from nine to six daily. When the war started he joined American Airlines, starting an economic research library for the company. He is still with that company, having held a number of positions. He is now assistant secretary of the corporation.

Mr. Paradis's mother, Marjorie Paradis, is a well-known author and through her he always had an avid interest in writing. One night in 1949 he dreamed he had written a book for boys on how to earn money. It seemed like such a good idea when he awoke the next morning that he hurried to the library and found that there was no book on the subject in print. A year later a publisher accepted his manuscript and a new career was started.

Adrian A. Paradis, and his wife, Grace, the parents of three children, live in Bronxville, New York.

you can sex
girl up